M000033224

Hello, Friends!

Stories of Dating, Destiny & Day Jobs

by

Dulcé Sloan

ANDSCAPE

LOS ANGELES NEW YORK

Copyright © 2024 by Estraya! Productions, Inc.

All rights reserved. Published by Andscape Books, an imprint of Buena Vista Books, Inc. No part of this book may be reproduced or transmitted in any form or by any means, electronic or mechanical, including photocopying, recording, or by any information storage and retrieval system, without written permission from the publisher. For information address Andscape Books, 77 West 66th Street, New York, New York 10023.

First Edition, February 2024
10 9 8 7 6 5 4 3 2 1
FAC-004510-23348
Printed in the United States of America

This book is set in Baskerville
Designed by Stephanie Sumulong

Chapter 7 Image Credit: Comedy Central's "The Daily Show" used with permission. © 2023 Viacom International Inc. All Rights Reserved. All other interior images courtesy of Dulcé Sloan

Library of Congress Cataloging-in-Publication Control Number: 2023939100
ISBN 978-1-368-09550-1
Reinforced binding

www.AndscapeBooks.com

SUSTAINABLE FORESTRY INITIATIVE
Certified Sourcing
www.forests.org
SFI-01681

Logo Applies to Text Stock Only

Dedication

I want to dedicate this book to ME! And to anyone who doesn't think you can dedicate a book to yourself. I didn't think I could write a book. The process was hard. It made me cry, laugh, call upon my public school education, and question choices I made in my past. But I did it! *airhorn* I'm proud of myself and what I created and I hope you, the reader, enjoy it.

Contents

Such a Nice Lady

I t was 2022. The infamous NYE celebration featuring the once-a-year Don Lemon acting up and out. As we stood together on a sparkly float at the New Orleans New Year's parade, staring right into CNN's cameras, Don asked me my resolution for 2022 and I spoke up, actually more than once—

"No more broke dick!" I shouted! I was too fast for the censors! Well, you never know when you will be called upon to start a ministry, and that is mine.

Since I was very little, I've been a performer and a storyteller—a funny one, I'm told—and that's what I'm put here on Earth to do. My ambition is God-given. In these pages, I'm gonna give you the full version of my life, the one you won't get when some goofy-ass reporter is trying to tell my story for me, twisting it to make me seem like I'm some Angry Black Female Comedian just to get some clicks. My sanity is fully intact. I'm just trying to make sense of the world around me. Yet some folks cannot stand the thought of a Black woman with a microphone on a stage being herself and talking about her life. So think of this book as the me you won't get in interviews, or even on TV. It's Dulcé, unfiltered. Like a cool, refreshing beverage that's half-filled with liquor (like my personal favorite, soju).

I had C-cup boobs by the fourth grade, so if you couldn't see my face, I looked like a short, grown woman walking into my homeroom, like I was maybe a substitute teacher or a confused parent sitting down with the kids. Ask the man who hit on me in a Payless shoe store when I was NINE. When I turned around and he saw my face, that fool sprinted out of the door so fast, he looked like he'd just stolen some cheap pleather loafers. Grown men have been hollering, "Aye, miss lady!" at me since the Clinton administration.

That also means that since elementary school I've had to deal with people expecting that loud, scary Black woman when I walk into a room. When they want to say it in a *nice* way, they call me *intimidating*. Listen, I own multiple Cricut cutting machines! I've made wall art with song lyrics from my favorite female rappers, baby-shower gifts, and a custom cake topper for my thirty-seventh birthday. I craft. What is so intimidating about a Black woman minding her business and making custom gifts for family and friends?

If you're one of the people who finds me *intimidating*, you might be surprised to know that a lot of times, I am not remotely comfortable in the spaces or rooms I walk into. The minute I walk in, I'm always navigating through what people think I am. They may have preconceived notions, but I know damn well what and who I am. I'm a nice lady. I hold the door for people. I love to give compliments. I'm a whole person, not clickbait. Like the time I was on a SXSW panel with John Cleese and he went off on slavery and Reparations, trying to make a joke, and suddenly all the headlines were about Cleese being racist and "super cringey," and me firing back at him. Everybody turned me into—again—the angry Black lady, and wrote about the story with no context. Some people cannot see that, though.

Like a wardrobe lady who made me cry because she got the wrong size clothes for me, because she thought I was lying about my measurements. There is no point in lying to a wardrobe person, especially when you are plus-size. Those clothes were *two to three* sizes too big and they didn't fit. Instead of accepting her mistake and apologizing, she blamed me. Instead of getting loud and arguing with her, I went and cried in the makeup chair. The nice makeup artist had to console me. Luckily I already knew that trick where you put a tissue in the corner of your eye to catch the tears so you don't mess up your eye makeup, a la Candiace Dillard Bassett from *Real Housewives of Potomac*. I'm not indestructible. I'm still a person with feelings. So people should stop treating me like a damn iron lady. I'm not saying I'm a pushover, but I do cry in makeup chairs from time to time.

As a Black woman and a woman from the South, I was never really taught self-care. No one ever told me that my needs could come before someone else's. We're taught to do for others before you do for yourself, except when it comes to getting your nails and hair done. That is the limit. You cannot come out of the house looking crazy. Acting crazy, maybe. But do not have busted nails and raggedy hair when you do it.

This book is for anyone who has had to endure being marginalized and seen in a way they know isn't true—and not being able to do anything about it. Sometimes it feels like I'm supposed to represent everybody that looks like me, or represent *something*, when really I'm just here to tell some jokes. When y'all come up to me on the beach or after a show and say nice things, it makes me feel great. I especially love the people who tell me, "Dulcé, watching you helped me get through the pandemic!" That means a lot to me to hear, because I had a hard fucking time during the pandemic myself! I was sitting in my house trying not to die, same as everybody else. If seeing me perform helped anybody get through it, that's something I'm proud of. If you were buying up all the pajamas and alcohol, I see you. Comfy clothes and liquor have come to the rescue for generations.

I want anyone who feels marginalized or trivialized to be able to learn to speak up and say things you feel like you can't. Speaking up for yourself and others can have consequences, and no one knows it more than me. I have had to defend myself all my life. I'm good at it now! Or I try to be.

Sometimes, Black children aren't allowed to be children, and it didn't help that I looked like a mother of three by the time I was fifteen. My stand-up is usually about my experiences as a Black woman in America, and so some people call me a political comedian, but I'm just talking about my experience being myself in my body and walking down the street. I'm just telling stories as they happened to me. When you look like me, or maybe like you, everything becomes political.

I once saw a TikTok video where a woman said, "I am not intimidat*ing*, you are intimidat*ed*." It's not on me, or us, to make people feel better about who we are or what we look like or how we think. We all just want to be loved, and have nice things, and walk into a room and not feel like we have to prove we're "nice." I've spent my life standing up for myself, and I'm gonna tell you all about it, unadulterated, in the pages of this book. Are you ready? Get your comfy clothes and alcohol (if appropriate). Let's go.

ONE

A Cornflake
Is Born

If you translate my first name to Modern English, I am Sweet
Lazarus Sloan. *Dulcé* means "sweet" or "candy" in Spanish,
for those who don't know the basics of the language that 43.2
million native speakers know in America. With a name like that,
I was either meant to be on a stage, or I was meant to be a pimp
in a 1973 Blaxploitation movie. Either way, I was *not* meant to

work in an auto body shop or a stucco supply company (even though I did both of those things, because I had to eat and I like to live indoors).

I was born on July 4, 1983, at 6:53 p.m. (or as my mother says, "Seven minutes before seven") at the Baptist Hospital in Miami, in the room above or below where my mother, Mary Ann Hill, was born twenty-one years earlier. I was named after a Cuban woman named Dulcé who went to cosmetology school with my mom. I guess she made an impression. As for Lazaria, it's the feminine version of Lazarus, and my mom and my aunt just liked it.

My mom couldn't decide whether my first name should be Dulcé or Lazaria, and she kept going back and forth until a nurse gave her the birth certificate and said, "Ma'am, I'm not bringing this typewriter back up here. Dulcé is your daughter's name."

So some random woman in Miami who finally put her foot down decided that my first name was Dulcé. Thank you, ma'am, and God bless. I don't know if I have what it takes to be a "Lazaria," but it would have gone well with my brother's name.

My brother is named Lawrence and he was born on Thanksgiving Day 1984, in Oklahoma City, just like our father. (My mother says God gave her children holiday births so she could remember our birthdays.) He was named by our father. Lawrence was *his* father's name, and he passed away before either of us was born. Since I was small, my nickname has been "Duce," because I've always had thick legs and my mom's oldest brother once said I was built "like a deuce and a quarter," which is another term for a Buick Electra 225. The nickname stuck.

Yes, my uncle, my grandmother's oldest child, nicknamed me after the nickname of a car. A car that got *its* nickname because it was 225 inches long. Good people who have read this book thus far, why was this allowed to happen? Was I not a wee babe, sir?! Your only sister's firstborn! I was also told I had ham hock legs, so as nicknames go, I think I came out on top. My family still calls me Duce, or they call me by my last name. I swear my mom has cousins who don't know my actual real name.

By the time I started kindergarten, I had lived in Miami, Oklahoma City, Colorado Springs, and Atlanta—in that order. My mom and father split up when we were in Oklahoma City, and my mom took me and my little brother to Colorado Springs because she had a homegirl there. I haven't talked to my father since about 1986. Lawrence calls him our "progenitor" instead of "Dad," like he's some kind of clone from a *Star Trek* episode. So that'll tell you about all you need to know.

We lived in Colorado Springs from 1985 to about 1988, in a blue split-level house that was in the middle of a hill with a steep incline. My mom started dating a man named Kenny and he lived with us too. I don't remember much about him, but I do remember my brother and I called him "Kenny Daddy." I do remember sitting on the stairs in the house and him doing my hair. He must have taken good care of us if we gave him a name like Kenny Daddy. I always wondered if we were told to call him this, or if my brother and I just made it up. I asked my mom, which I should have done years ago instead of pondering it all these years, and she said we came up with it on our own. We moved to Atlanta a few months before I started kindergarten because one of my uncles lived there, and Kenny Daddy didn't come with us. My mom told me it was because he didn't want to leave Colorado, which I could understand, but how different would my life have been if he came with us to Atlanta? What if we stayed in Colorado? What if I had a father growing up? Okay, this is too deep. This is a book by a comedian and I am that comedian. So yeah, let's move to the next paragraph.

In 1989 I was six years old and we lived in a suburb of Atlanta called Austell. It was then that I decided what I wanted to grow up to be—number one: An Actor, and number two: A Wife and Mother. Not a comedian—an *ACTOR*. I'm talking theater, summer stock, and Shakespeare. My dream job was and is to be a Klingon on *Star Trek*! And I don't mean the new *Star Trek: Discovery* Klingons, I mean *Next Generation, Deep Space Nine* Klingons! Worf, son of Mogh! Martok, Chancellor of the Klingon Empire! Me! Wearing a long, wet-n-wavy weave with titties poppin' like the Duras Sisters! Maybe there were times that I thought about doing something else: Chemistry? Archeology? Marine biologist? But I'm not great at math, so acting stuck. I couldn't do shit else and also be happy.

I wasn't exactly shy growing up. Once when I was at the doctor's office as a kid, I was clicking and clacking around in my sandals pretending to tap-dance, and a woman looked over and said, "You're very good." I looked that woman dead in her face with a big smile and said, "And I never even had a lesson."

I guess I have always had a big personality, which is a nice way to say I have always been A LOT—loud, outspoken, too much. But that's what got me to where I am today. Being "a lot" also helped me develop my talent for making grown men, teachers, and other adults question themselves when they tried to make me question who I am and belittle me, which is a trait that was and is a BLESSING.

In October 1992 we moved back to Miami. We lived with my Grandma Beulah and then we lived in a luxury hotel in North Miami Beach called the Marco Polo Hotel with a kitchenette in the room and a shopping mall on the bottom floor. We were there because my mom's dad was in a nursing home nearby and she was his caretaker. My mom paid one of the housekeepers to watch me and Lawrence when she was at work. One day this woman asked me and Lawrence to clean up our toys, and I looked *her* dead in her face and said, "Clean up? But isn't that *your* job?" I wasn't trying to be rude, but my mom was mad as hell when she found out. My mom told me she had to pay the housekeeper extra that week so she wouldn't tell the hotel that me and my brother were there by ourselves. But the woman DID clean hotel rooms as a job, so was I being too much, or just honest? Or both? This is the story of my damn life.

We were learning Spanish in school, but my brother picked

up a little German from the German tourist family at the hotel. This family taught Lawrence how to swim. Every day we went swimming, either in the pool or the ocean. We stuck mainly to the pool, though, so the hotel staff could keep an eye on us. The German dad, a full-bodied man who wore a Speedo, yelled, "Swim, Kinderlein, swim!" until we paddled hard enough not to drown. I spent so much time in the pool that my hair turned green. And yes, a little Black girl's relaxed hair can turn green! My mom swore she could see the green tint when the sun hit my head.

When I was in the fifth grade in the fall of 1993, we moved to a suburb of Miami, where I started attending a magnet school. This was the second time in my life I could take the school bus to school because we actually lived in the district (yes, my mom would use somebody else's address so we could go to a better school. Didn't your mom? That was the true mom hustle). In fifth grade I was tested for the gifted program. And by "tested" I mean I was asked to do a series of puzzles. I guess I'm good at puzzles, because I got in. And to this day I love solving a mystery. Especially a murder mystery. Not a true-crime murder mystery; I don't want someone to actually die. I want an actor to pretend to murder someone, and then go home to their family at the end of the day.

The best thing about the magnet school was when I started singing in the chorus. I wanted to do the theater program as well, and I thought my audition went well, but for some reason the teacher didn't like me (*cough* racism). Not because of things she said, but by the way she talked to me. It was an attitude. Plus, my mom told me this teacher was racist, and I trusted my mom. And no, I'm not trying to give an excuse as to why I didn't get in. By the time a Black child is ten years old they are fully aware of the hateful and racist glare of a white adult.

I did love chorus. All you had to do for the audition was sing "Happy Birthday." Nailed it and got in immediately. That chorus room turned out to be the perfect stage, and I was glad to perform, glad to spend a couple of hours singing my heart out. One day I forgot to tell my mother I had chorus practice after school. That might not seem like a big deal, but when I didn't get off the bus at home she went into a full-on panic. Fun fact: Florida has one of the highest missing-child rates in the country, and my mom loved to remind us of it. She even said there was a point where, as a kid growing up in Miami, she couldn't even play in the front yard because children were being snatched like clockwork, every fifteen minutes. It didn't help that I had the body of a grown-ass woman. So anyway, I'm singing my heart out in chorus, and I hear my mom's voice come over the school PA system: "Dulcé Sloan, please come to the office!" You know it's bad when you hear *your mother's voice* on your school intercom. What the hell—did she wrestle it out of the principal's hands? When I get to the office, she's in tears and the principal is *furious*. I didn't even get to hug my mom before the principal started berating me.

"Where have you been?"

"I couldn't hear you! I was singing!"

There was a piano playing and about twenty-five kids singing "Frère Jacques," so of course I didn't hear her. Then, after getting yelled at by my mom *and* the principal, I had to go back to chorus rehearsal. I hadn't seen my mom cry since her dad's funeral, and that day she was inconsolable. But she soon figured out a way to make sure it wouldn't happen again; she started working at my school. She got the job simply because she came into the school community computer lab one day to print a résumé, and they were like, "Oh, you know how to print a résumé?" And they hired her on the spot.

The day I called my social studies/language arts teacher a bitch (under my breath!) for some reason I can't remember, the time between me getting in trouble and my mom whupping me was less than an hour. My principal was more than happy to call my mom to her office, tell her what happened, let my mother whup me in the school bathroom, and then send me back to class. My mother always says I was good at cussing, but back then she wasn't having it.

Eventually, me and my family finally left Miami and went back to Atlanta. I can tell you I was the strongest little girl you have ever seen, lifting moving boxes and hauling furniture through two states. I could have tried out for *American Gladiators*, I swear.

Going to five elementary schools, two middle schools, and one high school, across two different states, was not my favorite thing. You lose friends all the time. I didn't even have friends until seventh grade, when things settled down. I didn't want to leave Miami, because I thought it would be cool to grow up where my mom grew up, plus you are never cold in Miami and I appreciated that. But there were too many hurricanes and not enough jobs in Miami.

My mother made sure that we went to good schools. We always lived in good areas, but we went to even better schools. So imagine my surprise—the true clutching of plastic childhood pearls—when we returned to Georgia and I had to go to school in the City of Atlanta for the spring of my sixth-grade year. It was not anything like the suburbs with its gifted program, up-to-date textbooks, and actual school supplies. All the kids at this city school told me I "talked white," which was wild to me because I went to school with kids of various racial backgrounds who spoke just like me. On day one they were like, "Why do you talk like that?" And I was like, "Talk like what?"

I was a suburban kid in the 'hood. This was during the Clinton administration, and our social studies books only went up to President Carter. Reagan wasn't even in the damn things. The maps in social studies still had the USSR on them. And what is Rhodesia? A country? A classmate? I was at a magnet school a month ago. What was happening? My history teacher taught from memory, I swear. I knew Reagan and Clinton existed, so I went home every day mad as hell and asked my mother when we were moving.

"Gimme a second, Duce. I'm trying."

"Okay, but WHEN ARE WE MOVING?"

There was a girl at school named Wendy . . . Wanda . . . Wilhemina . . . something with a *W*. She would walk around the halls looking for other girls to fight, and this kid Darryl would tell her who to knock out. One day they walked up to me and I was like, "What do you want? And who is he?"

"He's my agent," W said about Darryl.

"Girl. Are you okay?"

I did not know what else to say to this girl who thought a five-foot-two kid named Darryl might actually be her agent. I was actually worried about her.

She was there to start trouble with me. I had on a leather-and-cowrie-shell necklace that my mom's friend made me, and I loved that thing. It was a big deal in the 1990s; everybody from Lisa Bonet to James Van Der Beek had one. *And* Dulcé Sloan. So when W reached out and broke my necklace, I saw red, and I knew I had the full ability to stomp this whatever-the-fuck-her-name-was girl, maybe because of all the moving boxes I hauled as a kid.

I *knew* I could fuck her up, but if I did that, I'd have to keep fighting people, because that's how this school worked. All these kids surrounded us and she punched my arm, but I didn't feel a thing. I wanted it to be over, so I sighed and kneeled down on the ground, holding my arm, pretending to be hurt.

I was mad as hell, but I knew that this was the best option for me if I was going to survive this awful-ass school. She punched my arm again and started talking shit, but I was just waiting for it to be over. Looking back, maybe this was one of my early acting triumphs, because W and Darryl believed that I was down for the count. When I got up, Darryl was like, "You know she just got to be fighting and stuff." I did not want to get suspended and get in trouble at home for punching this girl in the head, so instead I *acted*, I played the role of W's victim, and then they left me the hell alone.

The first few weeks at this school, I was so unpopular that I once had lunch *with a teacher*. Have you ever seen a movie where the cool kid has lunch with a teacher? Me neither. I didn't win any friends by playing dead and letting W and her tiny agent get away with wrecking my necklace. Eventually some girls in my homeroom started being nice to me, probably because they felt sorry for me. Once they got over the "talking white" thing and I got good at playing the card game Tunk, we were cool.

This school in Atlanta was so messed up that it still had corporal punishment, and not just from W. Some of the classrooms were in a big metal trailer, and the kids were so wild that the math teacher would stand outside with three yardsticks taped together, the science teacher was there with a switch, and the social studies teacher, who was on crutches, used those crutches as a weapon. The math teacher would just stand there, smiling, waiting. So if you were running or acting up, you'd have to pass through a gauntlet of yardstick-switch-crutch as punishment.

It was wild. But there was a reason for it. There were kids that would run back and forth opening and slamming shut the doors to our classrooms.

One fine day I was walking into homeroom and someone slammed the door shut on my hand. I screamed and fell to the ground, but only the girls I played Tunk with seemed to be concerned. My teacher feigned an attempt to look out the door and find the culprit, and instead of really looking for the guilty party, she just sent me to the nurse. My mom had to come and pick me up and take me to the doctor. They removed my nail, put my finger in a splint, and sent me on my way. My ring finger is STILL flattened out to this day, but I can't be too mad because whoever slammed that door probably got caught in the yardstick-switch-crutch gauntlet for running past those doors.

Finally, the summer after sixth grade, we MOVED! I changed schools, back to suburban Atlanta, to Norcross, where I stayed until college. There were maybe seven other Black families, two white families, an Asian family, and a Puerto Rican family in this apartment complex. Ninety percent of my neighbors were Mexican and El Salvadorian. I was already bilingual thanks to the Spanish classes I took every day at school in Miami. I used to help the neighbors who didn't speak English register their kids for school or translate documents for them. Since I already looked like a grown woman, the adults often thought I was the kids' mom. I was like, what the fuck are y'all talking about—these kids are Mexican and I'm a child *and* Black! But big boobs will fool all kinds of people, especially dumb people.

Take Mrs. Wilson. That woman despised me—I still don't know why. To be honest, it's a little weird and unsettling to be a fourteen-year-old and know your freshman biology teacher, a grown woman with a job, HATES you. Bitch, you're forty-five years old! Why're you picking on a damn kid? But Mrs. Wilson made it clear as hell she didn't like me. She was always trying to call me out for talking or being disruptive, even when I was just sitting in my seat and minding my own business. For example:

"Dulcé, stop talking," said Mrs. Wilson.

"Dulcé is not talking. Leave Dulcé alone," I replied.

She 100 percent had it out for me. Once again, it wasn't what this teacher said, but *how* she said it. She snarled and hissed, I swear to God. She also singled me out when the entire class was talking and I was minding my business. Mrs. Wilson taught our gifted science class, and I knew I belonged there because, in the words of Sheldon Cooper from *The Big Bang Theory*, "My mother had me tested." I did all the fucking puzzles in the fifth grade to prove it, and here she was trying to kick me out, for what?

Eventually Mrs. Wilson got her way because she used a bullshit excuse to kick me out of class. The school had come up with a new policy about student schedules that was so convoluted; I am doing you a favor not even going into it. Just know that Mrs. Wilson got rid of me, and as much as I disliked her, I hate hate *hated* my new schedule. There was also no space for me in one of the new classes I was moved into, so I had to sit in the teacher's office with the door open so I could hear. Even the teacher felt bad for me. You were supposed to be better, Gwinnett County! I thought I left that nonsense in the City of Atlanta. But once again: Tomfoolery. Shenanigans. Hijinks. But I had nice books and shit.

I walked by Mrs. Wilson's class on the second day of my second semester of my freshman year of high school, popped my head in, and yelled, "I'm gonna be back!!"

My friends started yelling and cheering, and Mrs. Wilson goes, "No, you won't." So I gave her a dirty look, said, "Yes, I will," and I went on to my theater class.

When I told my mother what happened, she told me I had to handle it. She said I had to fight, and she used examples of times she had to go up against white teachers when she was a kid. And she went to a segregated school until she was ten years old. So I was definitely sitting at the feet of a master. My mother had given me the tools and the motivation to fight my way out of this unjust situation. The other thing that motivated me was the busywork. I hate doing busywork. It's a waste of ink, paper, and intelligence.

The next day I went straight to Ms. Landry, the head of the gifted program, and started doing one of the things I do best: going toe-to-toe with a grown-ass adult, pleading my case, and asking lots and lots of questions.

"So why is Vincent allowed to be in honors math and gifted science, but I can't . . . ?"

"Well, Dulcé . . ."

"Explain why Taylor is in gifted math and honors science. . . ."

"Dulcé, let me expl—"

"My cousin has gifted biology and regular math, and so do Lena and Gordon. I've counted seven kids with gifted biology and regular math, so why am I being singled out? Either y'all have got to put me back in that gifted class, or you've got to change seven people's schedules. The rule applies to everybody, or nobody."

"Who is your science teacher again?"

"Mrs. Wilson."

"OH! Her. Yeah. . . . You made some valid points. Let's change your schedule. And I look forward to having you in my English class your junior year."

Ms. Landry was cool, and she knew, like all the kids and the other teachers knew, that Mrs. Wilson was not good with students. So she granted my wish.

I walked into Mrs. Wilson's class again on Friday afternoon.

"Dulcé, what are you doing here? This isn't your class."

"Yes, it is."

I put my schedule on her desk. "Ms. Landry signed this." And then I took my seat.

All the kids were clapping and cheering. You know the meme where the young Black man with the glasses is smirking at the camera while his friends are jumping up and down? It was like that, and that bitch was MAD. I could see it in her beady eyes.

I could never understand why she was so mean to me or why she was so unpleasant to the other students. Later that semester we had a substitute teacher who had known Mrs. Wilson for years, and this sub told us that Mrs. Wilson had been pregnant nine times, but her white blood cells would always attack the embryos, and so she couldn't have kids. It suddenly all made sense why she was so mean all the time. She spent her days staring at other people's successful pregnancies. I don't know what kind of gossipy-ass sub would share personal information like that, but it did help me understand why Mrs. Wilson was so mean. It didn't make me love her or anything, but I understood. I could see why she'd be pissed.

Two years later, she had my brother, Lawrence, in her class. On the first day of school I popped my head in the classroom, pointed at Lawrence, and yelled, "That's my brother! Have a good afternoon. . . ." I was hoping she wouldn't treat my brother the way she treated me, but alas, she wrote Lawrence up one day for "making gang signs with his hands" when he was making a peace sign. My brother defended himself to his administrator by saying, "I wasn't throwing up the Crip, I was throwing up the hello."

The hardest part of being a young Black woman in high school was having to constantly defend yourself. I cared a lot about school, and Mrs. Wilson wasn't the only teacher I had to go toe-to-toe with to get the education (and recognition) I thought I deserved. I also had to battle it out with my tenth-grade

Gifted Language Arts teacher, Ms. Brown, who tried to give me a failing grade on a group project because, according to her, I had "copied my work from the other group member." If it's an assignment that is done with more than one person, how could we all write down different things? We did the work together! Also the "group" was just me and another girl, named Molly. But I guess she couldn't call it a "couples" project. I asked her how she determined that I had copied the work and my white partner had not, and she didn't have a real answer. I had to fight tooth and nail just to get a C when I should have gotten a B like my partner did.

"Ms. Brown? Why did I get a zero on this and Molly got a B?"

"Because you copied Molly's work."

"I didn't copy her work. We worked together. It's exactly the same work."

"Well, it should be different."

"Why would it be different if we worked together? And why do you think I copied her, and she didn't copy me? That doesn't make any sense."

"Dulcé . . ."

By this time, I was crying.

"Ms. Brown. Either we both get a B, or we both get a zero. That's fair."

"Fine," said Ms. Brown. "You'll both get a C."

Molly was not happy, but at least I didn't have to go home and tell my mom I got a zero.

Lawrence had Ms. Brown two years after I did, and apparently they liked to roast each other. One day Ms. Brown called my brother a hoodlum, and he came back with, "You're so old, you begat Abraham." She was so upset she left the classroom for the rest of the period, and never messed with him again. Now I'm not saying I'm happy she was upset; I'm saying that folks need to stop messing with Mary Ann Hill's children.

Now remember that before all this, back when I was six years old, I had decided to be a performer. I took theater classes, I was in chorus, and I took a few dance classes, too, all to fulfill my dream of being a working actor. The only time I thought about doing anything besides acting was when we learned about archaeology on PBS and I thought that might be fun, until I realized I'd have to get dirty. I did not want sand in my hair, so that career was out.

Then I thought maybe I'd be a marine biologist and work with dolphins, until I realized how much math you had to learn. Dolphins don't do math, so why the hell is there so much math in that field? And I loved chemistry. All the experiments and colors were cool, but then there was weird math. Half of that shit has to be made up. What y'all need all that math for? Huh? But the urge to pursue acting stuck.

My first part in a full play was when I played Bailiff Number 1 in *Arsenic and Old Lace* my freshman year of high school, the fall of 1997. It's a comedy about two old ladies who poison people to death. I only had a few lines, but I was so proud and excited you would have thought that I was starring in the show. It just confirmed that this was exactly what I wanted to do for the rest of my life.

Sophomore year I was cast in a bigger role as the Fairy Godmother in the musical version of *Cinderella*. This was the year after the movie with Whitney Houston and Brandy came out, and I was playing the same role as Whitney Houston. That song "Impossible"? It's almost impossible to actually sing. I wore a blue dress, blue house shoes, and a blond Dolly Parton wig, even though you'd think my mom would have gotten me a Whitney Houston wig. Walt Disney would have lost his mind if he saw me.

I remember the theater teacher telling me other people wanted this role, but she gave it to me because she thought I could do it. Each semester in high school I would rotate between the regular performance class and musical theater, and by the second semester of my senior year I starred in a very little-known musical called *Starmites*. It was an off-off-Broadway show that eventually made it on Broadway about a shy teenager named Eleanor who creates a fantasy world involving science fiction characters in her comic book collection. She escapes into her fantasy world, where the Starmites are the guardian angels of Innerspace. I played Diva, the bad guy, and I had a group of henchwomen called the Banshees. I made a necklace out of plastic cocktail knives and put on long, freaky red nails, so I definitely looked the part. I even made knife necklaces with color-coded beads for my henchwomen. But because it was my first starring role, I got so nervous that I lost my voice. I was sucking on lemons and drinking salt water, which was counterproductive, but what did I know then? By the last show I was able to calm my nerves and sing the songs full out. I remember only some of the words now, but I fully remember the feeling of singing on that stage.

During my four years of high school, we had three different theater teachers come and go, but no one could tell us why. The school was in a nice area and the students were very dedicated to the productions, but something was up. My favorite of all our theater teachers was my last one, Mr. O'Neill. He was a very nice, short man who was all about business and didn't take shit from anybody. I respected his commitment, but most of the other kids hated him for some reason. Yes, we were doing *Starmites* and we did a show called *Runaways*, but we also had no budget (which was very suspicious because Gwinnett County Public Schools had lots of money), so he had to find plays that didn't have expensive rights or production costs. I was always defending him to my friends and fellow officers in our International Thespian Honor Society, saying that he was just trying to do his job. It felt different defending a teacher since I was usually trying to defend myself against a teacher, as if we were on opposing teams. At the end of the year he gave me a star-shaped paperweight as a gift, for supporting him throughout the year. And to this day I still have it.

Not all teachers had it out for me, but I remember every single one who did! Going back to 1996, I remember one teacher in seventh grade gave me a "nine" on a math test, and when she handed me the test, I laughed.

"Are you laughing at your grade?" she asked.

"Yes!"

"Dulcé, you need to take this seriously."

"But it's a nine! And I worked through every problem. And I got every answer wrong. Why didn't you just give me a zero?"

"Because you attempted every problem. I gave you half a point for showing your work."

"BUT IT'S A NINE!"

I know she was trying to be nice by giving me some credit, but I couldn't help but laugh. It was a nine!

My teacher insisted that I get the test signed by my mother. So I went home with my algebra shame to see what punishment I would face at home. When my mom got home from work, I told her the news.

"Mommy, my math teacher wants you to sign my test."

"Why?"

"Because I got a nine."

"Out of ten?"

"Out of a hundred."

"What?!! Hahahahaha!"

"Yes, ma'am!"

"AND YOU ANSWERED EVERY QUESTION??"

"Yes, ma'am!"

"AND YOU GOT A NINE!"

And then we laughed for the next five minutes.

"Why didn't she just give you a zero?"

"That's what I said!"

And then we laughed some more.

"Mommy! Can I put it on the fridge?"

"Absolutely!"

The next day, my math teacher asked about the test.

"Dulcé, did you show your mother your math test?"

"Yes, ma'am, I did."

"What did she say?"

"She laughed."

"No, she didn't. Bring the test back."

"She did laugh. And do I have to bring it back? We put it on the fridge."

"Y'ALL PUT IT ON THE FRIDGE?"

"Of course we did! I got a nine!"

"Never mind."

That math test stayed on our fridge until I graduated college.

Fast-forward to my junior year AP Economics teacher who we called Coach because he was the school golf coach. I didn't know we even had a golf team. Apparently they won championships and shit! Coach kept trying to teach us about supply and demand, which was some Santa Claus made-up bullshit if I had ever heard it. I tried to listen, but one day I just couldn't take it anymore. If the demand is higher, the price goes up. Okay, but why? How is all of capitalism based on this? I will twerk with a unicorn at a leprechaun's quinceañera before this shit ever makes sense.

We kept going back and forth until eventually I was like, "Whatever, Coach."

"Whatever, Coach? That is your argument now?"

"Either I cuss you out and get suspended or I say 'Whatever, Coach.' I'm choosing whatever."

"Yeah, you would get written up," he said before he shook it off and continued with his class.

He passed me with an eighty, which was a B. Technically I had a sixty-nine in the class because I never understood what the hell was going on, but he "didn't believe in grades that ended in nine," so he bumped me up to a seventy. And with the ten points added to the final grade because it was an AP class, ya girl was blessed with a B. I had him again my senior year for AP Psychology and AP Sociology. I had grades in the nineties before the ten-point bump because the classes made sense! He gave me an award for Sociology at the Honors Award Ceremony that year. I asked if I had the highest grade, and he said no. "You're the only one that's engaged in what we're talking about, and I'm tired of seeing the same kid get all the awards. He has the highest grade in the class, but he doesn't care about the material." Coach is the only high school teacher I still talk to on Facebook.

With all that work, I made my mama proud and got a full ride to Brenau University, a private women's college in Gainesville,

Georgia. I was really looking forward to my college theater experience because I wanted to learn all I could about my chosen profession—but things did not go as planned.

As a theater scholarship recipient, I was required to audition for every show. There were five shows a year, equaling twenty shows in your college career. I was in two of them. There were many performance majors who graduated without being in a single show because they were not one of the "golden children." The "golden children" were a group of overworked and never paid students handpicked and groomed by our head theater professor and program director. I used to wish that I was in this select group, but in the end it was a blessing. I learned that the disapproval and apathy of one white man will not stop me from achieving my goals and reaping the benefit of an $85,000 theater degree with no student loans. Praise God! Most of his "golden children" were so burned out by the end of college that they stopped acting completely.

I, on the other hand, am the most successful graduate of the program. Me! Ya girl! Look at God!

My acting classes consisted primarily of in-class scene work and journal entries. Our entire grade was *Zip! Zap! Zop!* Character work. And a diary about the class. No one really kept up with the journals. Typically a group of us would get together and write the night before they were due, and we'd ask the ONE person who actually did their journal entries after every class to help us, to make sure we all got our stories straight. I got along great with the other students. I was doing well in my technical theater classes because I learned so much from my internship at a community theater. And I *thought* I got along with my theater teacher. So I was truly surprised, confused, and hurt when I found out that this grown-ass man had some kind of issue with me. (**sigh**) This shit again. I didn't want to go toe-to-toe with Mr. M. I was an eighteen-year-old freshman giving it my all in a damn theater class, and he was a forty-five-year-old man with a wife and children. He was supposed to teach me, not destroy my confidence.

At the end of the first year all of the students had an assessment. We sat down with the three professors in the theater department, and they let us know how they thought we were doing in the program. I thought that's what grades were for, but what did I know? My other two professors, one of whom was Mr. M's wife, had nothing of real note to say. "You are doing so well in this, improve in that, *blah blah blah*. More *Zip!* Less *Zop!* Your *Zap* is perfect!" I remember every one of these sessions feeling slightly awkward, which made sense because it was an awkward situation: three grown adults judging children who are pursuing their dreams. That shit is weird. I had done theater competitions and auditioned for my scholarship, but this was different. This conversation had the power to change the course of my life. I had heard from upperclassmen that the assessment had made students change majors or quit the program altogether. I was determined not to let that happen to me. I knew I was talented and that this degree was gonna be free. So they were gonna have to put up with my Black ass until graduation day.

The assessment was going pretty well—some praise, some goal-setting, some basic constructive criticism. The last person to speak was my acting professor, Mr. M. He started by saying the usual, "You are doing so well in class, *blah blah blah*." I thought we were about to be finished, but then his tone changed. "But, Dulcé . . . I feel like I don't know who you really are. . . ."

I was floored.

"What do you mean?"

He sat up as if he were a therapist diagnosing my problem.

"Dulcé, I feel like who you are outside class and in class is different."

"Professor," I said. "No one is the same in class as they are out of class. Are you the same at home as you are at work?"

"Well, maybe it's because you moved around a lot and had to learn how to fit in quickly."

In the first few weeks of class we had to do a journal entry about our childhood, and this man had chosen to use my words and life against me. But, like he said, he did not really know me, and he definitely didn't expect me to come back at him after that bullshit.

I responded with, "That's interesting, sir. Because I don't know who you are either."

One of my other professors chuckled and quickly cleared her throat.

"I'm sorry, what?"

"I see three different Mr. M's. There is one for the students, one for the faculty, and then there is MR. M HEAD OF THE THEATER PROGRAM for the donors and the endowment fund."

He blinked. I blinked. His wife's mouth was wide open with a look on her face that said, *Oh shit, she gets this man.* That was the day he was done with me. And I mean done. He didn't speak to or really acknowledge me for the rest of the year, even in my Acting I class. He did shady shit to me all throughout my sophomore year, including trying to miss my second year assessment. He showed up very late, but I was still there because I was crying in front of my other two professors trying to figure out if I needed to transfer because I was so unhappy with the program. They told him this and he said nothing. When I told my mom she said, "Girl, don't let them folks stress you. Get your degree. Where else are you gonna get a free ride?" Great point.

Also I LOVED my college. I was elected by the other freshman students to be in the Miss Brenau pageant. I didn't place, but I had a great time. I was active in a lot of the clubs and activities on campus. And I really liked that I was at a small women's college. But I was struggling in my major. My junior and senior years I didn't get cast in any shows. My freshman year I was in the children's show written and directed by the theater director's wife, and my sophomore year I was in the spring musical, *Ragtime*. It required a large Black cast, and at the time there were only

five Black people in the theater program, and four of them were
women, so they had to cast all the other Black cast members from
actors out in the community. Smart programming for a season,
right? I was cast as "Sarah's Friend" who had a big solo at the
end of Act One. Mr. M didn't let me sing the solo. Instead, he
gave it to a woman from the community whose only role in the
show was to sing my character's big solo—much to the confusion
of the musical director, choreographer, and everyone in the
show. When one of the other Black girls got sick and couldn't
perform, he had no issues asking me to fill in her singing parts
because I "wasn't in those scenes and they needed an alto." Like
I said, shady shit.

By the time I got to my senior year, I was ready to be done. I
was the Secretary of Membership for Alpha Psi Omega, the
theater honors society. I did fourteen scenes from the one-woman
show *Fires in the Mirror* by Anna Deavere Smith for my senior
thesis performance in the fall so that my spring would be smooth
sailing. I had a great time during school. I was a peer advisor
to the class of 2007 and made sure they stayed focused and
productive and out of trouble, so no one ended up murdered,
like the plot of a Lifetime movie or on the news. If you have
ever had to watch over a group of drunk sorority girls in various
frathouses, it is truly like herding cats. I had a radio show on
our college station. I rode mattresses down the stairs of various
dorms and sorority houses. I helped some friends take over
student government only to have them stop talking to me a year

later. To this day I still don't know why those girls stopped talking to me. I'm sure one of them heifers will read this book and let me know with an apologetic but passive-aggressive Facebook message. Girls, if you are reading this book, please know from the bottom of my heart and the depths of my soul—fuck you! What you did was unnecessary and hurtful, and I will give you detailed MapQuest directions on how to kiss my ass. I know I should be the bigger person, but you should have apologized when George W. Bush was president. Stop it.

I didn't sign up for assessment my senior year because I didn't want or need one. I saw other students hugging and having tearful goodbyes with our professors. I knew that I wouldn't have that experience, even though I wished I could. These were the last formal teachers I was ever going to have, and all I could think was, *What did I do that was so wrong?* What was it about my existence that vexed them so much? But as with any other conflict with power-tripping authority figures, I had to realize that their issues were none of my business. I had learned from my thirteen other years of school that sometimes, people just don't like you. And there have been people I just didn't like, so I get it. BUT I wasn't their teacher *or* an adult. And I would never so willfully shut out an ambitious and bright child because I had some personal issue of my own.

I had to get my transcript signed by Mr. M so I could graduate. I walked into his office, handed him the form, and said, "I don't think we have anything we need to talk about, do you?" He signed the form and said, "Nope, we don't." I walked out of his office and the next day I walked across the stage at the Georgia Mountain Center to receive my diploma. A bachelor of arts in theatre performance and an incomplete Spanish minor. It was incomplete because the last class was in Spain. SPAIN! The country! Nobody told me that when I signed up for my minor! I couldn't afford books, so how the hell was I gonna get to Spain? ¿Cómo? ¿Con una bicicleta? ¡Déjame! I got an $85,000 theater degree with no student loans and zero debt. The Lord had truly blessed me. I can finish that Spanish minor at any time. (I *still* don't have that minor.)

I did learn one important thing from Mr. M, so I'll give him credit for that ONE THING. He would always tell us that we were artists, but we were also cornflakes. Like the mass-produced and brilliantly marketed cereal. We are a product that is bought and sold. Your headshot is the shiny picture on the box and your résumé is a list of ingredients. And he was absolutely right. This shit that I do, and that any performer does, is at its core creative.

But we can never forget that this is a business. And the hardest part is remembering that. We pour our heart, soul, time, money, and bodies into performing, and not everyone reaps the rewards at the level of working full-time. But those of us that succeed must always be wary of the agent, manager, booker, and other industry persons trying to pimp our dreams and goals. People love to justify the toughness inherent in this business.

"Oh, you're a performer. That is *so* hard. Y'all face so much rejection." I really need people to stop saying this, and for performers to stop internalizing it. What we feel when we don't land a job is an emotional and visceral response. But that's it. You just didn't get a job. Applying for any job is hard. No one is telling people fresh out of accounting school that the world is full of rejection if they didn't get a job at the firm they applied to. So why do performers have their feet held to an emotional fire? It has always felt manipulative to me.

When I first went to Los Angeles and started meeting with agents, they would say all the usual: "Dulcé, you're a star," and "We're gonna make you a star," or whatever they learned in agent school to make performers feel all pumped up before shit gets real. Maybe they expected me to smile and nod and thank them a thousand times for paying attention to me. But instead I said, "Thank you, but as much as I am an artist, I am also cornflakes. So how are you gonna sell me better than all the other millions of cornflakes out there?"

After three meetings there was finally an agent who knew what I meant. He smiled and said, "She gets it." And I signed with him that day.

Fast-forward again to almost two decades out of college. I've got a great career, friends, and family, and I'm working full-time as a performer. I go on trips to Hawaii and Turks and Caicos, and I get my hair and makeup done to go on *RuPaul's Drag Race*. It is not a bad life. I'm out here making people laugh, acting, having a good time, and doing what I said I wanted to do when

I was a little girl. That theater professor may not have wanted my brand of cornflakes, but I wasn't going to allow the opinion of one man to change how I viewed the goals for my life. Maybe he really wanted some bland-ass oatmeal. Or Cream of Wheat. Or any other breakfast food. But the rest of y'all are eating it up. Thank you. Truly. I'll never forget that what I have and who I am is special. You will always come across people who want to offer their opinion of who you are and what you "should" be doing with your life. But the longest relationship you are ever going to have is with yourself.

So do whatever you can to make sure that your opinion of yourself is the most positive, most supportive, and most loving it can be. Speak life into yourself. Stop saying you are a "starving artist." People starve to death. Why are you saying that the life that you want is slowly killing you? You are speaking death into your goals for your life. Change the way you talk about your future. And then figure out how you gonna pay the bills. 'Cuz, friends, living inside is expensive.

TWO

No One Said
I Couldn't Do It

I t might not be a surprise that my mom encouraged my
practical dreams, like becoming a young flea market
entrepreneur or singing in my school chorus. What might surprise
you is that she *also* supported my dreams of being an actor. From
a young age, no one told me I *couldn't* make a living doing one

of the toughest jobs in history to actually make a living at, so I figured, why not try?

I didn't come from a long line of acting royalty. I didn't have an uncle who ran a major movie studio. There was nothing nepo baby about me. But even so, my mom never said, "Duce, that is the dumbest thing I have ever heard," or "Do you know how much rejection actors face? Go do your math homework!"

She said, "You want to be an actor? What are you gonna do to make that happen?"

"I don't know, Mommy. Act cute and get on TV?"

I had so much to learn.

Maybe I decided to become an actor because I watched Nell Carter on the sitcom *Gimme a Break!* She played a—wait for it—housekeeper for a white man who was a police chief. In my defense I didn't realize that she was a housekeeper. I just knew she was in charge. I was six. I remember seeing reruns and thinking, "I could do this!" That was the first time I'd seen anybody on television who looked like the women in my family. We're not tall, but we are bougie. Nell Carter looked familiar to me *and* she was funny. I didn't actually get big until I was eight years old, though. It's in my genes. My mom and brother blew up at eight years old, too. There was a significant difference between me at six and me at eight. The weight came on and NEVER WENT AWAY. It's like one day I woke up and it just appeared. Whatever gene causes that to happen, my family has it. I don't know if that's what happened to Nell, but I looked at her on that TV screen and saw a familiar face.

In the 1990s there were a million Black people on TV. And plenty of Black women for me to idolize and admire. There was Queen Latifah on *Living Single*; *227* with Jackée Harry. I always liked Jackée Harry because her and my mom favored each other, as did both—yes both—Aunt Vivs on *The Fresh Prince of Bel-Air*. There was also *Martin*, *In Living Color*, *The Cosby Show*, *A Different World*, *Amen*. I loved *Amen* and *A Different World* because they showcased my first TV crush, Bumper Robinson. I loved the man. Also, Arsenio Hall had a talk show. We were always big fans of his show because my uncle Stevie B performed on the show in 1991. No wonder I thought I could be on-screen. My uncle did it, and I was gonna do it, too! How was I supposed to know it was gonna get canceled three years later?! I thought Arsenio's show would be on forever.

The reality of my school was a little different than 1990s TV, though. Let's go back. Long before Brenau, I was at my third and predominantly white elementary school in Sandy Springs, Georgia, a suburb right just north of Atlanta. We put on a Thanksgiving play and all the Black kids played Native Americans—and those were not the lead roles. Everyone in the South, Black or white, thinks they have Native American ancestry, so it worked out fine and no one was offended, as far as I could tell. They gave us the most fake-ass "Indian" names. I was Sparkling Water. I had maybe two or three lines, but I didn't mind. I was ONSTAGE. Technically I was in a classroom, but my mom came to see the play. She has never been a picture-taking mom, so there are no photos of me as a young Black Cherokee child. As soon as I got to high school and got my own camera, I carried that thing around with me everywhere to make up for all the pictures that were not taken throughout my childhood.

My mom didn't take photos, but she did support my dreams. In fifth grade I went to a magnet school in Miami, which had a solid theater program. This pretty Cuban girl was the star of the program, but when I auditioned, I still had high hopes. I was ready for the theater director to tell me that I was the most talented child actor she'd ever seen and that I'd be replacing the Cuban girl as the lead in every single production or working alongside her. After the auditions, she walked up to me and told me the good news: that I could be in the theater program! ". . . as a lighting tech," she added.

Oh.

I was disappointed, but I figured just being in the program I could find a way to showcase my skills. I had plenty of time for my big moment to happen, so I went home and told my mom the good news.

"Mommy, I got into the theater program."

"Good job! Are you going to be in the next play?"

"No, ma'am. I'm doing the lights."

"What do you mean you're doing the lights? That is not acting."

"I'm gonna learn about the lights and the sound."

"You are *not* doing no lights! You are a performer. You go

back and tell that woman no. This is some racist bullshit."

"But, Mommy . . ."

"My daughter is not doing no lights."

At school the next day I told the theater teacher I would NOT be doing the lights.

"Why not?" she asked.

"My mom said so."

"Why?"

"She said, 'My daughter's not doing no lights.'"

So instead of hitting light switches, I switched lanes and that's when I joined the chorus. My mom taught me an important lesson that day: Don't let racist magnet school theater directors crush your dreams. Go sing instead. I also learned how to play some instruments, so if you need someone to play "Hot Cross Buns" or "When the Saints Go Marching In" on the recorder, I'm your girl. I am sure casting directors all over the country have been searching for a grown woman who can do just that. Whoever you are, hit me up.

I loved theater and music, but PE and I were not on good terms. I have been wearing a bra since first grade, and they don't make sports bras for children. By the time I got to middle school, all the girls would lie and tell the PE teachers we were on our periods because then we could sit out and still get a good grade. It was the best. Have you ever seen a sixty-year-old man react to a twelve-year-old girl saying the word "period"? They freeze up, cover their ears, and sing "Lalalala!" at the top of their lungs before they turn to stone.

Every time this happened, I would think *You are a freaking health teacher! You teach kids about menstrual cycles. Why are you acting like this? Didn't you fight in a war?* But I never said anything because the excuse always worked. As long as I didn't have to run, they could be as ignorant and misogynistic as they pleased.

One day during high school, though, we got a new, female PE teacher. She noticed a bunch of us sitting on the sidelines and walked over to see what was going on.

"Why aren't y'all running?"

In unison, we yelled, "We're all on our periods!"

Instead of turning to stone, she rolled her eyes.

"Get up."

"But, Coooooaach! We have cramps! And my boobs are too big to run."

"I will tape your boobs down for you if you don't get up and run."

"But what about our periods?"

"I'm on my period, too. Get up."

"What are y'all doing up? Aren't y'all . . . on your . . . um, special time?"

"Yes, sir. But Coach Stephens said we have to run," I said.

Male coach turned to female coach in utter confusion. "They can't run on their *periods*."

"What? Yes, they can. Did they tell you that?"

We all stood behind him like he was defending us from the grown woman who was telling the truth. A few of us took his hand or held his arm. We looked up at him with our sweetest faces and biggest eyes, batting our eyelashes and sounding as helpless and pitiful as possible. "Tell her we can't run, Coach Robby. Tell her. We have cramps. And we're tired. And our backs hurt. And we have headaches. And it's hot out here."

"Well, umm. They have cramps and are tired and in pain. And it *is* hot out here."

Coach Stephens let out a big old sigh. "They can take some aspirin and sleep when they get home. There is no biological reason they can't run."

"What? Really?"

"I'm a health teacher," she said. "And so are you! They are playing you. They are on their periods, not nine months pregnant."

"If you say so. I'll let you handle it." He looked over at us, shrugged his shoulders, and walked away. Damn it! We were definitely running laps now.

"Nice try, ladies, but it's over," she said. "Give me four laps around the track. There's nothing that you can't do ever! Not even on your period."

But I *hated* running. It was my goal to go on record as achieving the longest mile in the history of the school. If the track stars ran five-minute miles, mine would take thirty! Once I just sat down on the track and people started yelling at me, but I reminded them I was trying to set a record. I don't have proof, but I'm pretty sure I did just that.

Unlike gym class, theater inspired me. I loved everything about it, and I did well and got solid A's. When we moved to Gwinnett in the summer of 1995 I started at a new middle school, where instead of giving an F grade, they'd give a U for Unsatisfactory. Maybe because the word "Fail" was too real? Too raw? Anyway, I got my report card and saw a U next to Theater Arts, and I *knew* it was dead-ass WRONG. My theater teacher loved me and thought I was very talented, so why did I, ME, get a failing grade? I ran to the theater to find out what the hell happened.

"Excuse me, but why did I get a U? I don't deserve a U."

She looked at the paper and blushed.

"I must have put in the wrong grade. I'll fix it on the next report card."

"In six weeks?!"

"I can't change it before then."

"No, ma'am," I said in panic. "My mom will kill me. You have to change it, or write a note. She will murder me in my sleep."

I begged for some kind of proof to show my mother that this was a mistake, but she refused. Probably because she didn't want to get caught for mixing up my grade and Jorge's grade, because his name was right above mine in her grade book. This kid Jorge always failed theater. He was a gangbanger-looking dude, and I would always look at him and ask, "Jorge, why are you here?" He was as interested in theater as I was in gangbanging. I never saw him again after that year. Maybe he moved, flunked out, or went to juvie. I know for damn sure he's not performing in a local theater production of *Hello, Dolly!*

That day I went home terrified to show my mom the report card. I walked inside and found her on the toilet peeing. I thought it was the perfect time to share my news—when she was physically and emotionally vulnerable.

"Mommy. Here's my report card. My theater grade is wrong."

I handed over the card.

"What do you mean the—"

Her eyes bulged out and she flew off the handle, and almost off the toilet.

"How are you supposed to be an actor with a failing grade in theater!"

"It's a U, not an F. . . ."

"It's the same thing!"

"It's a mistake. The teacher mixed up my grade with Jorge Salazar's grade because his name is above mine in her grade book. I asked her to write a note or change it, but she said it'll be fixed on my next report card in six weeks."

My mom handed back the report card, finished peeing, and glared at me like she *would* murder me in my sleep if I were lying.

"The next report card better be different."

I swear my mom gave me that same glare on and off for the next six weeks until the grade was fixed, which it was. Praise the Lord.

My freshman year of high school I was in a chorus show where we did selections from *Guys and Dolls*. I sang the song "Adelaide's Lament" as a solo. It's a song that says an unmarried woman could develop various ailments like a cold or the flu while waiting to find a man who will marry her. That's the basic premise, and presently realistic as hell. At that time, I loved halter-top dresses and the color blue, so my mother made me a blue sequined halter-top dress with a white sequined collar and waistband. My mom decided that if I was going to play a 1930s lounge singer, I needed to look the part. So we went to a theatrical supply store and got a long cigarette holder with a fake cigarette that had red reflective foil on the end to look like a flame. Puffs of smoke even came out when you blew into it. Onstage, it really looked like I had a lit cigarette. She made a ponytail and did my hair. This was the actual start of my mom being extremely supportive of my dreams. She always backed me up, but now she was sewing, buying props, and creating looks. She wasn't a stage mom, she never pushed me, but she made sure I had all the support I needed, and the right hair, makeup, and wardrobe.

I had my "Adelaide's Lament" solo, but my first *big* acting role happened sophomore year. The theater teacher, Mrs. Newman, was a white lady who really wanted us to know that she adopted Black children. She told us all the time and we were like, "We heard you, woman. But what does their hair look like?" It was the late 1990s. You know what their hair looked like.

She cast me as the Fairy Godmother in *Cinderella* in the fall musical, so because of that I had to end my line of questioning about her kids. I hope they all turned out well.

The Fairy Godmother was a huge role for me, and my mom came through with a blond wig that would make Dolly Parton and Miss Piggy wonder if the hair was TOO close to God. Remember that televangelist Jan Crouch, with the big blond hair that almost looked lavender? The wig was like that. I still have it. This role made me so nervous I almost lost my voice again, like when I played Diva in *Starmites*

I wanted to be good, and I wanted to hit those notes. And finally, with enough practice, I did. My mom got me light-blue slippers that matched my dress perfectly and were very comfy to wear. I got on that stage and belted out "Impossible" in my Jan Crouch wig with no nerves or flubs, and I made myself and everyone else proud.

My high school was voted one of the most diverse schools in America by *USA Today*, so no one questioned the casting choices. Colorblind casting was an everyday thing for us. There would be a cast with a Black dad. This role was played by a teenage kid who got his hair cut like Sherman Hemsley from *The Jeffersons* to imitate male pattern baldness—talk about dedication. That kid would wear a cap when he wasn't onstage to hide what was going on on top of his head, God bless him. In the same play there was also a white mom, an Indian daughter (South Asian), and a Black son. We were Shonda Rhimes's dream come true. It didn't even faze us. So once I got into college and then the "real world," I saw that, long before *Bridgerton*, colorblind casting in my world really only happened at Meadowcreek High School in Norcross, Georgia. Imagine that.

During my time at Meadowcreek, my mom continued to support me and help me with costumes, hair, and makeup. She was like my personal stylist, only a stylist who could ground me. When I was in the chorus for *Once Upon a Mattress*, a play that sounds like highbrow porn but that's really a musical version of *The Princess and the Pea*, I wore a pink dress with electric-blue pantyhose. The teacher wanted shocking colors when we lifted our Victorian-era dresses during one of the dance numbers, and my mom came through once again.

Our theater teacher my senior year, Mr. O'Neill, had us put on the play *Runaways*, which was a musical about kids who were living on the streets. It didn't do well on Broadway, but it was cheap to produce (we wore rags) and the teacher was very much about this indie shit. Also, the school had about a five-dollar theater budget. We were playing homeless teenagers, so we had to look dirty, like we'd just slept under a bridge. I came home and told my mom about the costumes for this play.

"I need to look dirty. Ripped clothes, stains, no sequins, beads, or wigs."

"That seems sad. What kind of play is this?" she said, but she still helped. She wasn't thrilled about it, but we got through it.

My mom supported me when I was in *Starmites*, she cheered me when I lost my voice and got it back again, and she never, ever suggested I stop messing around with theater and focus on something more practical. There were a few times she didn't back my dreams, though. Back in freshman year of high school I'd asked her if I could be in the color guard, spinning flags and doing dance routines out on the field. I figured it would be fun. I figured she'd support me.

"Mommy, I want to do color guard."

"The what? No."

"Why not?"

"You're an actor, you don't have time to be twirling flags."

So that was the end of the discussion. Jump to 2013. Me and my mom are in the front of her house. My brother is raking the yard and my mom and I are sitting in her car, and for some reason, I got curious about her banning me from the color guard back in high school.

"Mommy, how come you didn't let me do color guard? Was it because of the football players?"

She looked over at me and narrowed her eyes.

"Football players? Girl. I was supposed to spend my gas money driving you around so you could twirl a flag? There's no future in that! You can't get a job twirling a flag!"

"What?"

"What kind of job were you gonna get from twirling a damn flag? Huh? Were you gonna go from office building to office building raising their flag every morning? That's not a salary position."

She went on a fifteen-minute rant about the color guard, I swear to God. It may have even been twenty minutes. She was *still* livid.

"What I look like wasting my gas for you to twirl a damn flag?"

She did hate wasting gas. Color guard wasn't my life dream, and I wasn't devastated that she wouldn't let me do it, but still. Some parents might say the same things about acting: there's no future in it and it's a waste of gas money. Not my mom. She saw a future in acting for me! Or I thought so. A few years after college, when I was working odd jobs and doing some local theater, my mom decided to lay this one on me, out of nowhere:

"Dulcé, maybe you should have double-majored in business. . . ."

Excuse me, ma'am? Why did she wait until *after* I got a theater degree to come out with this practical advice? Where were you eight years ago, woman?

One thing my mom did NOT say to me:

"You should send your résumé to Tyler Perry!"

I am not fucking joking, friends. I heard this so many times, as if Tyler Perry just sits up in his Atlanta studio compound between Zoom sessions with Meghan and Harry, reading résumés and saying, "This guy works at Chili's, but he played a tree in *The Wizard of Oz* in sixth grade. Send him to me!"

Eventually I did get caught up in the Atlanta phenomenon that is Tyler Perry. Around 2010 they were looking for extras, and I submitted my headshot and résumé to the casting director. I was cast as an extra on his show *Meet the Browns*. It felt like every other Black person in Atlanta had worked for Mr. Perry in some capacity. My mom was even an extra in *Madea's Family*

Reunion. She didn't want to be an actor for a living, but she was having fun. I was doing small roles and extra work not to have fun, but to put my theater degree to use and start a career.

Eventually I went through that rite of passage that every young actor goes through: getting scammed by an "agent." I had to pay one hundred dollars to sign with this guy who told me he could get me big roles and make all my dreams come true, or whatever bullshit he fed me that I believed. I was new at this, and I couldn't yet see that the man was a con artist. As soon as I swiped my credit card, though, I was like . . . wait a minute! What is happening here?! It was too late by then. He had my money, and I had a thief for an agent. It was some bullshit. I got conned! Once my mind cleared, I called and had the charges reversed. While I waited for a real agent to come along, I did some lifestyle modeling. You know the kind of photos that show regular-looking people modeling in Advil ads or banners in Walmart or the bank. I was the woman in photos that showed the world: "Hey, we're a multiracial couple opening a checking account! Look at this mixed family getting on this plane! Check out this Black woman taking aspirin!" That was me. Living my regular life in a still photo hoping people will buy whatever I'm trying to sell on this coupon in a box of relaxer.

Through all those years of grinding it out doing extra work or small parts where I had one line, I would be what is known as "second team." That basically means stand-ins for the lead actors. You're picked because you're the same general color, height, and body shape as the lead, so while the crew spends eighty hours lighting a shot you stand there as if you are the actual actor so the actual actor can grab a croissant or smoke a cigarette or get a massage in their trailer. Maybe I didn't have a lead yet, but I was on a set, making my way. I was acting, sort of.

Through the grace of God I won a stand-up competition called "NBC's Stand Up for Diversity." It started twenty years ago as a way for NBC to launch the careers of comedians from diverse backgrounds, and for up-and-coming comics it is a big, huge, massive deal. After I won, I moved out to LA in 2016 to push my career to the next phase. During my first pilot season, which is when potential new shows are shot and judged to see if they'll become actual full series, I booked a supporting role in a pilot. Supporting role or not, this is also a very big deal. I booked a pilot my very first pilot season! Li'l ol' me! A lot of pilots don't get picked up to become a series, and that show was one of them. But I got to work with some amazing actors and I made the director, Amy Poehler, laugh, so that was amazing.

The last time I'd worked in LA was when I did an African Pride hair commercial, so speaking of getting a role in *any* pilot, plus an Amy Poehler pilot, was a major step. This was no Hooters commercial (I did those, too). With this pilot, I also had a holding deal with NBC, which meant that they were going to help me find *other* shows to be in. I was so nervous when we started shooting that one day I spilled apple juice on my shirt and panicked. The wardrobe girl came over with some kind of magical sponge and wiped it right off.

"Calm down," she said. "Are you a theater kid?"

How did she know??

"Yes."

"Y'all are all freaked out about eating in your costumes, and you always hang your clothes up."

She was right. I was trained to hang my costume up at the end of rehearsal or a show because nobody else was going to do it.

After the apple juice incident, the pilot went well and I put some money in the bank. Since the show didn't get picked up, I had to move on to the next project and get back on the road. In the midst of moving to LA and being in my first pilot, I was still performing stand-up comedy at colleges on the East Coast. I didn't have time to dwell on what didn't happen, because I had to move on to making the next thing happen. That's part of being a performer, so after that first pilot season, I came back for more.

In the spring of 2017, my second pilot season, I booked a lead role. Not a funny sidecar of a friend, but a LEAD. I showed up to set on the first day, got my makeup done, and when the assistant director called, "Second team to set!" I got up and started to walk to set. It took a minute before I realized, wait a minute. That's not me. I'm not second team. I worked as a stand-in for years on various projects. But not this one. I'm not doing the lighting, or standing in the background of another Tyler Perry show. Once I realized this, I started tearing up. The wardrobe head was a sweet Colombian woman and we called each other *prima*, meaning cousin. She saw the tears messing up my mascara and asked what was wrong.

"Prima, what's the matter? Why're you crying?"

I whispered, "I'm not second team."

"Qué? What do you mean?"

"They said second team and I stood up and then I realized they weren't talking about me. I'm first team. I've never been first team before."

"Congratulations, prima. Look how far you've come! Ven. Let's get your makeup touched up."

She whisked me off to the hair-and-makeup tent to get touched up.

As I wrote this I teared up again. It's been almost six years since I had that conversation, but the feeling is still fresh. I still remind myself I'm not second team. After driving all over Atlanta and Los Angeles going on auditions, and being in this or that off-off, not-even-in-the-Broadway-zip-code play, there I was.

I met the girl who was my stand-in, my second team, and she thanked me for the opportunity, as if I cast her in this second team slot. But she was right. Because I was cast, she got an opportunity. I recognized her excitement, though. I'd been there not long ago. In 2005 I got a theater degree from college, and in

2016 I was in Los Angeles doing an Amy Poehler pilot for NBC called *Dumb Prince*, which was about a reluctant prince who was too dumb to know how to run the family business, so he threw their lives into chaos. It was a big moment for me. A lot of that came from my own determination, and from my mom never telling me I *couldn't* make it to that point. That pilot didn't get picked up either, which was for the best. . . .

THREE

I Keep a Job

I got my first taste of real success at an open-air flea market in 1993 in Florida City, Florida. My mother would wake me and my brother, Lawrence, up every Saturday at the fresh dawn of a new day so she could set up her booth and sell her kids' clothing line, Dulcé Fashions. She also sold bundles of hair. CBS would play cartoons on the radio for some reason, so while she set up, me and Lawrence would sleep in the car or listen to my favorite cartoon, *Garfield and Friends*. I loved Garfield. I had more than one Garfield birthday cake and I always made sure to save the little figurine that came on the cake.

I would help my mom by walking around the flea market, modeling her fashions, and sometimes having my hair styled with the hair extensions she sold. My mother was a trained cosmetologist, so I would have all kinds of French rolls and finger waves. I mean executive realness. I was a young businesswoman on the rise, and I looked cute. I'd convince people to come over and give us their money in exchange for a printed halter top and matching pants or a cute dress. It was the 1990s, so every little Black girl in America looked like a grown woman. By the end of the day, my mom would make enough money for bills or groceries or more material to sew more clothes. She worked in the community center at my school during the week, but the weekends were her chance to pursue her passion. Her work ethic, her talent, and her desire to make extra cash rubbed off on me. I had ambitions, things to do, and money to make.

I wanted my own business, my own brand. I was ready to be a self-made woman when I was still a little girl.

I told my mom about my plans. Did she laugh, pat me on the head, and tell me I was adorable? No, ma'am. She went right out and got me a little fanny pack, a receipt book, and a few dollars so I could give people change. She even made up SKU numbers so I could keep track of my inventory. I started selling wholesale toys, like cheap plastic water guns and dolls, at the booth next to my mother.

The nice white man who ran the flea market let me use that empty booth for free. On some days, he'd take some of the kids riding around in his golf cart. One of those days, he drove four of us kids to this little shed-looking building on the property. He pulled up to this shed, and I got very uncomfortable. I don't know if this man had ill intentions, but when you combine innocent children with a grown man and a creepy shed, you get trouble, or murder. I didn't need Whoopi Goldberg to pop out and say, "Molly. You in danger, girl." I remember thinking, *Nope, sir, we are done here.* The man was probably just turning the cart around and the shed happened to be there, but I told him I wanted to go back to my booth and to my mama. That was the first time my woman's instinct kicked in, and it would not be the last.

When I started my cheap water gun and knock-off baby doll empire, my mom gave me business advice, woman to woman. She was dead-ass serious, telling me that if I was gonna do this, I was gonna DO THIS. This wasn't Girl Scouts, or a janky lemonade stand. If I was starting an enterprise, I was not going to listen to Garfield in the car and pray the toys sold themselves. I was going to commit. So I did, and damned if I didn't learn the value of a hard day's work. During my flea market days, I would make maybe twenty or thirty bucks on a good morning. I was so happy that I had a little business, just like my mom. It took a while to go from nine-year-old South Florida toy mogul to *The Daily Show*, but really, the Florida City flea market is where I got my start. It just took me *a lot* of jobs and a lot of paycheck stubs to get to where I am now. And I do mean a lot.

I've had so many jobs over the years, I can't tell you about all of them in these pages, because if I did, you'd be holding a fifty-pound book. Also, I can barely remember all of the jobs I've had, that's how many there were. Long John Silver's, Value City, Victoria's Secret, Bennigan's, Kroger, Old Time Pottery. I've managed and done concessions for small theaters and worked in bilingual customer service—I got great at being proposed to in Spanish when a man wanted a discount on his stucco. I've heat-pressed NFL logos onto hats, had a custom gift and jewelry business, did crafts at kids' birthday parties, and worked at a power company. You see what I'm saying? I've seen people lie, cheat, and skim off the top. I might not have been the best employee, but you know what? I keep a job. For the most part.

After college, I had two months to find work because my mom wanted me to start paying rent. One job I got was at a used car lot in Tucker, Georgia, in the summer of 2005 where I didn't get paid unless they sold a car—which is not what I was told when I was hired. I was told I would process paperwork and help the Spanish-speaking customers and would get paid commission once a week. They didn't tell me that they could go weeks without selling a car. That meant I made no money. The "employees" would have to follow these guys to a check-cashing place to get our pay. That's how shady it was. I told my mother this and she said, "Oh? I'm on my way."

Not only were we at a check-cashing place, we were at a check-cashing place in a liquor store. Pure class. My mother was more than a little upset. And when I got back in the car with maybe $150 after a week of work, my mother turned to me and said, "They need to find a better way to pay you, because we are never doing this again." I swore she was going to cuss me out, but I think she was just glad I got any money at all.

The owners of the car lot looked like henchmen in a movie. One was tall and slim and resembled a snake, so I'll call him Cobra. The other was shorter and built like a potbelly stove. Cobra was a real gentleman, because one day he told me if I wanted things to go better for me at work, I'd have to sleep with him. To which I said, "I don't think so, sir." What I really wanted to say was *Bitch, I'm a college graduate with skills, so get the fuck out of my face!* But remember, I keep a job, so I just thought those words, silently.

Cobra and Potbelly would send me over to competing used car lots to "help"—aka steal their leads—along with another employee I'll call Dead Tooth. A lead is a potential sale. People would come into the dealership and fill out applications, and I was supposed to take them. Dead Tooth was less creepy than Cobra, but still very inappropriate. To the point I had to threaten him with bodily harm at work. After that we didn't have any more problems.

Dead Tooth was my crime coach, showing me how to steal

the leads and why you needed to bounce around to different lots so the people working there don't realize what you did. I hated it and didn't want to do it. Also Dead Tooth kept getting caught, so I couldn't trust his guidance. Plus, this was too much work when the most expensive car on these lots was maybe $5,000 to $8,000. I think I was making 5 percent commission. All that for maybe $250 didn't sound right. A few weeks later I was "working" at a competing lot with Dead Tooth when me and Nelson, the owner of the competing lot, got to talking. Nelson was nice for the most part, he had a family, he wasn't at all creepy, and he would buy me lunch or give me a few dollars for gas because he knew I didn't have it.

I told him ALL the nonsense I had been through with Cobra and Potbelly, and how lecherous Dead Tooth was, so he offered me a job. He would say I reminded him of his oldest daughter, so maybe that was why he took me in. We both agreed I couldn't sell water to a man on fire, so selling cars was out of the question. He hated doing loan applications and paperwork, and I figured out the online system, so we made a deal. I would get paid hourly and get commission off a sale. Nelson also told Dead Tooth to leave me alone. Dead Tooth would later go on to steal a Jeep Cherokee right off Nelson's lot in the middle of the night. As the saying goes, "It be ya own people."

I knew I would have to go see Cobra and Potbelly again because I needed to get the last payment they owed me. I brought along my mom and brother as backup, just in case. Cobra and

Potbelly were not budging. They claimed they didn't owe me any money because Nelson was giving me money for gas and food, which means that Dead Tooth was not only a thief but a snitch! Of course they owed me money. They said they would pay for being at the other lots, and now they were backing away from that. Break bread! The fuck?!? Gimme my coins. I was on the phone with Nelson trying to get some advice, but he eventually said he couldn't help me and hung up. My brother left because he had to go to work, so it was just me and my mom, having a showdown with Potbelly and Cobra.

When I start jobs, I keep my head down, stand back, and observe, so Cobra and Potbelly always thought I was a nice, quiet employee, never causing trouble. That is probably why Cobra thought he could take advantage of me. No, sir. Not today. Not ever. When they wouldn't even give me the time of day, my mother stepped in. She went back and forth with both of them, and when Cobra realized he was losing with my mom he tried to reason with me because I was "nice and quiet." I am nice and quiet. When I want to be. But once he got rude with me and then my mom, it was over. He got in my mother's face and said, "I'm not gonna keep going back and forth with you, I need to talk to my nice and quiet employee."

"My daughter? Nice and quiet?"

"Yeah, nice, quiet, and polite."

My mother turned and looked at me, smiling. "Okay, go right ahead."

"Thank you!" He scoffed when he turned from my mother and then came at me with more confidence than he deserved. Now, my mother knows her daughter and she knew that this man had only met "work Dulcé," not "real Dulcé."

"Now look, you been working for me for a—"

"No, lemme tell you something, you bitch-made mother—"

I will spare you the rest of what "real Dulcé" said, but he was thoroughly cussed out from here to kingdom come. The surprise on that man's face. It's like when the nerdy girl gets the makeover and all the boys in school can't believe their eyes. *That* face. Once he snapped back to reality he started to explain and defend himself. I wasn't listening because at that moment I decided that I was going to rob that man. He had my money. He told me he had the money but that it wasn't mine.

Like any self-respecting woman in the South, my mom carries a pistol, and I knew where it was in the car. But I also knew if I walked away to get it, he would walk away with my money. I turned and looked at my mother, and then looked at the car. Again to her and again to the car.

At first she didn't understand, so I did it again. Her eyes got big. She ever so slightly shook her head no. Again I motioned to her and then the car. Again she slightly shook her head no. And then she motioned to the road where a police car was coming down the street. I have never seen so many cop cars in a three-minute period. This was a good thing because I was going to put a gun in that man's face and take every dollar he had and take his shoes.

I counted about fourteen police cars out there, and that bastard was still talking. That's when I stopped motioning for the gun, because I figured all those police cars were a sign from the Lord, trying to knock some sense into me, and keep me out of jail. It was very clear that I wasn't going to get my money, and he made it clear that one of the reasons was that I wouldn't sleep with him. Sir, if I'm selling pussy you're going to have to give me more than 5 percent commission on a 1998 Honda Civic.

The next day, I went back to Nelson's used car lot. Mind you, this was my first real job experience after college, and I saw shady shit from day one. I stayed with Nelson for a while, but I did feel guilty having to repo people's cars. There was one woman who worked at a daycare, and she came in begging for her car back. I felt bad, but once I realized that this woman skipped out on payments all the time, I was like, girl. One time, and you have my sympathy. Four or five times, you might need to take a bus.

Nelson had me coming in early to open the business, and staying late to close the business. Worse than that, he started talking to me crazy. He was like an annoying dad. He had a daughter about my age, so he very much would give me dad vibes, and I did not need that. He wasn't paying me enough to open and close the shop *and* listen to his dad advice, so after four months, I left that car lot, too.

Around 2010, I was working in bilingual customer service for a power company in Florida that had about two hundred employees. I spent my days telling hundreds of people a week that I could not turn their lights back on—in English *and* Spanish. We were all based in Georgia, but on the phone we'd have to say we were in Florida because there was some company policy that said all of their employees had to work in Florida.

I got this job through a temp agency called Raybad. I never met my sales quotas for water heater warranties and some electrical insurance because I was talking to people who could barely pay their power bill, so why would I ask them to add twenty-five or thirty more dollars to their bill? I felt bad. The only way we could take breaks at this job is if we went out to smoke or use the bathroom, so there was a group of us that trained together and we'd coordinate our smoke breaks, which annoyed our supervisor, Miss Dana, because her whole team would leave at once and we'd stroll back in smelling like a pack of Newports.

One girl I worked with drove a Corolla with no power steering, so I told her she must be the strongest bitch in Atlanta. She had arms like Popeye, I swear. I bought a bunch of baby blocks at the Dollar Tree and told everyone that if they wanted to go on a smoke break, to put their block on top of their cubicle as a signal. In jobs like this you have to entertain yourself so you don't die of boredom, and I was the VP of Entertainment at every job I had. I wasn't pulling out a ten-piece marching band, but I did my best.

One day during one of our three-minute smoke breaks, I asked this girl who was the top salesperson how she did it. How did she pressure people who were struggling to pay. How did she convince them to pay *more?*

"I gotta get this money," she said. "I don't know them."

Fair enough, but hell is hot. She took a drag of her cigarette and left it at that.

When we got back to our cubicles, Miss Dana was not happy.

"All ten of y'all can't leave here at the same time," she said.

"Yes, ma'am," we'd mumble before we went back to our cubicles to wait until we could put our baby blocks up on the cubicle again.

One day we all went to Chili's for lunch and had margaritas. It took them forever to bring the bill, so we ended up being gone for over two hours. When we stumbled back in, Miss Dana was standing there, glaring.

"Where the hell have y'all been?"

"Miss Dana, we tried to get back but it took an hour to get our bill!"

"Just sit down," she said. "And next time y'all bring me back a margarita."

Miss Dana was all right.

At this time in Atlanta it was EASY to get an apartment. They literally had ninety-nine-dollar move-in specials. If you wanted an apartment with three tennis courts, multiple pools, and washer-dryer units, it would be about $450. I was making about ten dollars an hour and living in an apartment that was in a gated community, so I was doing pretty well. One of the girls who worked in the cubicle behind me was called Mud Duck. At least, that's what Popeye Arms called her behind her back and, when they would get into it, directly to her face. One day I took off work because I was doing extra work on the Tyler Perry show *Meet the Browns* (Miss Dana was cool like that), and when I came back all my coworkers ran over. Folks could not wait to tell the big news.

"Girl. Where were you yesterday?! You missed it!"

"Missed what?" I asked.

"Girl! Mud Duck got arrested!"

"What?!"

"They came to the office yesterday and handcuffed her RIGHT HERE!"

"And I missed it? What'd she do?"

The smile that came across Popeye Arms's face when she told me. Why'd she get arrested? I'm going break it all the way down for y'all. See, at this job, we would take people's credit card payments all day long. The boss made us put our phones away so we wouldn't put people's credit card numbers in our phones, yet we were told to write down the numbers with a pencil and paper so people didn't have to repeat the numbers and we could keep our call times down.

So we have to hide our phones or we will be fired BUT we can write down the numbers and y'all don't check and make sure we throw them away at the end of our shift? Cool, cool. Mud Duck was using customer credit cards to buy herself lunch every day. She had been doing it for months! Because who would really notice? Do you remember every time and every place

you grab lunch? Most people don't. The way I would know if
someone stole my credit card would be if there were a bunch
of charges to Wingstop, because I HATE Wingstop. What if
this stranger saw a bunch of charges for Arby's or Jimmy John's
and said, "Hey, I didn't make these charges. I'm a vegan!" But
that's not how Mud Duck got caught. Miss Thing went down
in a blaze of glory.

Mud Duck got caught because the goofy bitch also paid her
rent with a stolen credit card. It belonged to some man in Texas,
and his wife saw the charges and was probably like, "Why the
fuck are you paying rent in Georgia?!" That girl could have
wrecked some stranger's marriage. They eventually tracked it to
Mud Duck because the man called the apartment and asked for
the name of the person living there. All our calls were recorded,
so they had a tape of her talking to the man and getting his
credit card information. We already knew about the lunch
hustle because she was bragging to us about it one day, and I
specifically warned her that she was going to get caught. She
replied, "Nah, I'm good. I know what I'm doing. Ain't nobody
thinking about me." But somebody was! And that "somebody"
was the Fulton County police. The worst part of this story is
I MISSED HER BEING ARRESTED IN HER CUBICLE!
I always miss the drama at work, but I was trying to do something
for my career, working as an extra, so the sacrifice was worth
it, I guess. But still, they perp-walked this bitch and I did not
witness it! My parting words to Mud Duck would have been,

"Girl. Not everybody can do crime."

A few months after that drama wore off, I got a call from a payroll-deduction company I used to do bilingual customer service for, asking me to come back.

"I have a job," I told them.

"We'll pay you a dollar an hour more."

"I'll see you Monday," I said, because I am no fool.

I told Miss Dana that my old job wanted me back, and that I was going to start Monday. She reminded me that the policy of that raggedy-ass company was that if I didn't give them two-weeks' notice, they'd pay me $7.75 an hour instead of ten dollars an hour, to punish me. We all agreed to it when we signed the contract for the job, like a bunch of dummies.

"Dulcé, you've got to do what you've got to do," said Miss Dana.

It was time to go to my mom.

"Here's what you do," she said, like some kind of badass *Ocean's 11* character planning a bank heist. "On Monday you call the power company and tell them your car is in the shop, and you start your old job back. Keep doing that until your power company check hits the bank at midnight Wednesday, and then you can quit after that and still get your ten dollars an hour."

I am blessed to have a mama who is ABOUT. THAT. LIFE.

So that's what I did. On Monday I went back to my old job at the payroll deduction company and called the temp agency at the power company and said my car was in the shop and I couldn't come in. I gave the whole song and dance. "I don't have access to public transportation, no one can pick me up. . . . Blah blah." Tuesday I called them on my lunch break and gave them the same song and dance, and added that the mechanic was waiting on a part and I should be back to work by Wednesday or Thursday. A supervisor was put on the phone and insisted that the mechanic fax them a copy of the bill to prove that I was waiting for a part. Really? This fictional mechanic doesn't work for y'all. This is ridiculous. And two hundred people worked on my floor alone. Y'all have plenty of employees. So to continue this farce I asked for the fax number and pretended to write it down. I even asked the supervisor to repeat the number to make sure I got it right because I have a theater degree and this was the first acting gig I had had in a while. On Wednesday I received a voicemail from them stating they never got the fax from the mechanic. I called back on my lunch break, very apologetic. "But he told me he sent it. Can you give the number again?" Once again I pretended to write the number, and they warned that if I wasn't at work on Thursday I would be fired. I assured them that I would be there. And I had to be because my check was going to hit at midnight and I didn't need any problems. All I had to do was wait.

Midnight. My paycheck is in my account at my ten-dollar-an-hour rate. We did it. And I was glad I went back to the payroll deduction company. The money was better and the calls were easier, so it was a win-win. On Thursday the power company called me. They called me many times. Leaving voicemails asking where I was and asking why they still haven't gotten the fax. There was no fax, baby girl. It was all a clever ruse. And I never called them back. That night I went out with my homegirl to celebrate. When we got back to her house, I had a voicemail from the temp agency that got me that job.

"Hi, Dulcé, this is Tiffani from Raybad! I'm just calling to see what the status of your car is and when you would be coming back in . . . or [slight gasp] . . . wait a minute . . . or if you got another job and called out for three days so we wouldn't pay you minimum wage, but if that didn't happen, call me back!" Tiffani figured out my scheme WHILE SHE WAS LEAVING THE DAMN MESSAGE. I could literally hear her putting the pieces together as she was leaving the message. To this day I wish I would have saved that voicemail. I played it for my friends. Played it for my mom. Played it for my new coworkers, because it was magic. I would have made it my ringtone. I would have played it when I won an award as part of my acceptance speech. It was truly one of my proudest moments. But then I erased it.

A few years later I got a call from someone else at Raybad offering me another bilingual customer service position for twelve dollars an hour.

"Hello?"

"Hi, this is Melissa from Raybad. How are you doing today?"

"I'm good. Before we go any further, you should know I'm banned from working for y'all."

"What?"

"I'm banned."

"I don't see that in my system. Would you be interested in a bilingual customer service position for twelve dollars an hour?"

"I would be," I said in the driest voice because I knew this call was going to be a waste of both our time, "but I can't because I'm banned."

I heard her clicking away on her computer.

"Umm, let me call you back."

"Sure." I was looking for another job, so I was hoping and praying she actually wouldn't find anything.

Ten minutes later she calls back.

"Yeah, I don't see anything saying you're banned."

Ah, a glimmer of hope. Maybe Tiffani realized that the policies of her company were outrageous and she wanted me to have another chance.

"I will give you some more details about the company and set you up with an interview."

Hallelujah!

"Oh, wait," she said. "I see the flag."

Damn it, Tiffani! I knew there was a flag on my name! Of course there was a flag on my name! I'm sure there is a United Nations of flags on my name!

"This says you can't ever work for us again, you're permanently banned. I've never even seen this. You mind if I ask, what on earth did you do?"

I told her the whole story and she was actually pretty impressed. And she even laughed out loud when I told her about the voicemail.

"Well, that is amazing and hilarious and you are very qualified for this job. But I can't take the ban off in our system. I would, because of that story, but I literally can't. The system won't let me. But I have no doubt you will be fine. Bye."

"Bye." Well, shit.

One of the craziest jobs I ever had was around January 2006 working at an auto body shop where the boss, Catherine (who was also the owner's daughter), never trusted me with the financials, even after two years. She hired me because they needed someone who spoke Spanish, and we graduated from the same college, so I thought this job would be a lot easier than it was. They never had any issues with me, but she still didn't trust me. There were three locations—two in Chamblee and one in Duluth. By the end of my time there I worked at all three. There was a Laotian chick named Sally who worked at the first location, and Catherine trusted *her*. She had been working there for almost seven years and would go above and beyond for them when she didn't need to, but the way they kept saying they trusted her always struck me.

I worked at the smallest location, but I had more freedom than Sally and the girl at the third shop because we didn't do as much business as the other two shops. Catherine was a trip.

"Dulcé, I want to call my husband my baby daddy. Can I do that?"

"No, Catherine. No, you can't."

And sometimes she'd have me hold her baby while she took calls, and eventually I was like, "Nah, I ain't doing that mammy shit," and I handed the baby back. Unless the baby was crying real hard, I did not hold him, because then I had to. He was still a wee baby. Catherine was always comparing me to Sally and saying that one day she would show me all the stuff she was teaching Sally. Back-end financials, deleting parts and labor charges off of work orders, like real big-money stuff. I told her she could take all the time she needed because I had no desire to do more work.

Turns out Sally and my old coworker Mud Duck were two peas in a pod, because Sally got caught stealing $10,000! I said $10,000 American! She did it slowly, over the course of a year and a half. Catherine wouldn't tell anyone how she caught her. Sally was better at crime than Mud Duck, but she still got caught. Let's be real, if you are stealing from your job and it's through the computer, you are going to get caught. Right after it happened, me and the receptionist at the third location were on the phone for an hour trying to figure out how Sally pulled it off, but we never could. I called the first location and talked to two of the office guys up there for over an hour, and none of us could figure it out. Sally didn't get perp-walked because she had a rich brother who could pay the $10,000 back and keep her ass out of jail. She did get fired, though. Again, a gentle reminder that not everybody can do crime.

At the body shop there was a Vietnamese mechanic named Tu who escaped during the war. He had a thick accent, but I never had a problem understanding him, maybe because I always grew up around immigrants and because *he was speaking English*. Tu would always say there was more damage to a car because when he started taking the car apart, there would usually be additional damage that couldn't be seen by the insurance agent when they wrote the estimate. Catherine would tell him to work off the original estimate from the insurance company, but Tu would have to explain why he needed the supplemental estimate, and I would end up translating his English to a forty-year-old white woman, and then I'd have to translate her English back to him.

"Bumper no good. Need to be replace," Tu would say.

"What did he say?" Catherine would ask.

"Seriously, Catherine? He said the car needs a new bumper."

It would go back and forth like that until their discussion ended.

I was back at the shop later that day to check in parts, and Tu looked upset.

"Why she act like my English not good? You understand me. Why she not listen?" he said.

"Your English is good. She doesn't *want* to listen to you, Tu. That's the problem."

Now before we go hating Catherine, remember when I said

I had to translate her English to him? Well, the next day Tu comes back into the office.

"Estimate no good. Too much damage. Tell him come back. Need more time."

Catherine looks at me, confused.

"He said the insurance agent needs to come back and do a supplemental estimate. There is too much additional damage on the car. And he needs more time to fix it."

Tu nods his head.

"Well, Tu, the insurance companies really want us to work off the initial estimate. To try to keep the cost of the repair down."

Tu furrows his brow and looks at me. "What she say?"

"She say he not coming back. Insurance company say use first estimate. No more money. No more time," I replied.

Catherine nods her head.

"No, no. Need more time. More broken parts than first esti-mate. Headlight case, grille, front quarter. Tell her."

Now they both look at me.

"The headlight assembly, grille, and front quarter panel are all damaged and need to be replaced. He needs more time," I sigh.

"Hmm. Let me see the estimate." Tu hands her the paperwork and she looks through it. "Okay, we will reach out to the insur-ance company about writing the supplement and let you know when he is on the way. Tell him." She hands the estimate back.

Again they both look at me.

"We call insurance company. Tell them you need more time. I tell you when he coming back."

In unison they say, "Okay. Thank you," and Tu goes back into the shop. Catherine turns to me and says, "Thank you so much. I can never understand what he's saying."

"What do you mean?!" I exclaim. "He is speaking English!"

"Well, as long as you can understand him."

Every time this happened I would sit there, wondering what the fuck just happened.

I got up and went back into the shop because I thought my brain was going to explode, and I was truly worried I was being racist, when Tu walked up to me and said, "Thank you. I never understand what she say. Her English too complicated. I always understand what you say. You always help me."

"I'm glad to help and, yes, her English is too complicated."

"She say all those words for no reason, dah, dah, dah. Just tell me!"

Tu made me laugh.

Catherine was actually cool sometimes. She knew my career goal was to be an actor, not a cog in her family's automotive repair machine. She let me take time off to go do summer stock theater in the mountains of North Carolina, in a town that was so isolated it was about forty minutes from the closest Walmart. That's how I measure civilization, by how far something is to Walmart. The road to the town was so narrow you could reach out your car window and touch the damn mountain. I was playing

Tom Robinson's wife in a production of *To Kill a Mockingbird*, and while the play ran I lived in a house with the rest of the cast and crew. Catherine told me that if I trained a temp, I could take three weeks off as long as I came back. I made a huge training manual so this new girl would know exactly what to do. I trained the hell out of her, but when I came back after three weeks, Catherine and all the technicians were like, "We're so glad you're back!" I don't know what the hell that temp girl did to make them love me so much. Looking back over all my jobs, Catherine was one of the best bosses I had. She couldn't understand Tu or the concept of a baby daddy, but she was all right besides that. When my shop closed, I was moved to the third location up in Duluth and I hated it. I was trapped at my desk all day, and the owner and Catherine could see my computer screen directly from their offices. So I got a job at one of the car insurance companies we worked with.

A couple of years later in 2013 I was part of an improv group, and I started hooking up with one of the other members, Tommy. We rehearsed a few times a week in one of the rooms of a music studio in Atlanta. I was on unemployment because I had been laid off from another job, so I had lots of free time. One night we were all there hanging out, and the owner of the studio, Corey, asked if I knew how to use Microsoft Word.

"Of course I know how to use it," I said. "I'm a grown adult who works."

He asked me to fix all this paperwork he'd put together for a mentoring program he had, and from then on I kind of started managing the whole studio, because the men sure as hell couldn't do it. I remember on Martin Luther King Day we were all at the studio, and the one white boy who worked there was the only one absent. The owner, Corey, called him up, and the kid was like, "I thought we weren't working since it's MLK Day?"

"All the Black people are here! If we're not taking this day off, you can't!"

I swear.

I managed the studio, but I don't want it to seem more glamorous than it actually was. Corey's desk was an old door that he rested on top of two hobby horses. Also, when you're in a music studio you hear the same song ALL DAY LONG, over and over. It's not like I was in there with any professional artists, either.

When Corey wasn't mixing down a song or mentoring a student, he was flirting with me. He would kick in the door to our office and yell, "What up?!?" He'd make a lap around the room and then leave just to make me laugh. He had been flirting with me for months, but I didn't pay him any mind because he flirted with everyone and now he was my "boss."

I stopped hooking up with improv Tommy eventually because, well, he was homeless and had no job. When you say that out loud, it makes pretty good sense. But for him, that wasn't a valid reason. We were still on speaking terms, though, because we were in an improv group together and didn't want any issues. One night a girl I went to high school with was having a party at the studio. An ice storm hit the night of the party, so I ended up having to stay in the studio because it was late and I didn't want to drive. I just needed a place to sleep. There were multiple big couches, and Tommy and I had once hooked up on a futon outside of Corey's office bedroom, so I could have slept there. But on this particular evening, a new option arose. Corey's bedroom.

By now, Corey and I had been flirting for months. I knew he didn't have a girlfriend because his mother told me. I had to make sure before anything happened because HE told me he was a cheater, and I didn't want any problems. When I went inside, Corey was like, "Let's just go to sleep." He was high and drunk and I was tipsy and tired so we were legit going to sleep. We lay there watching Netflix, and then I realized I forgot I'd left my coat and my phone in the room where the improv group rehearsed, so I went down to get my stuff. At this point, the party was over, and I thought it was just me and Corey in the studio. I didn't know Tommy was still there because even though he had no home, he didn't stay in the studio *every* night. But there he was, awake in a chair.

"Where were you?" Tommy said. I felt like a teenage girl getting caught sneaking back in the house.

"Just upstairs," I said.

"You don't have any shoes on."

"Yeah, I was upstairs. I'm going to bed."

"Okay, let's go to bed."

So Tommy follows me upstairs, and the dude is literally

breathing down my neck. I felt like I was doing a death march. I had the option of sleeping on a futon in the cold with Tommy, or going into a warm room and sleeping on an actual bed with Corey. I had to crunch the numbers. Do I let Corey wake up in the morning and see me on the futon outside his bedroom with Tommy? Or do I get back in bed with Corey and deal with Tommy's feelings being hurt? The real question was: Do I get in bed with the man that owns the studio, or do I lie on a futon with a man who sleeps in the paint room and who I have already stopped hooking up with?

These were the thoughts racing through my mind as we approached the room. Once we got to the futon, I had to move as fast as I could, so I hurried into Corey's room and closed and locked the door behind me. I could hear Tommy breathing on the other side of the door for *a long time.* I was scared to go and get in the bed until I finally heard him walk off. I was worried he would make a scene or cause a big commotion, and I'm sure he wanted to, but he had nowhere else to go. Why would he piss off the man who let him crash in his studio?

I thought I was in the clear, so I lay down in the bed. All of a sudden, my phone blew the fuck up. It was vibrating so much that Corey woke up. Do you know how much a phone has to vibrate to wake a grown man up? Tommy was livid. I didn't even read the texts because they were so angry and I just wanted to go to sleep. Eventually the buzzing stopped, and I passed the hell out.

Tommy didn't come back to the studio for a while after that.

By the time he did, I was basically running the place. He came back to work here and there, and since I was running shit I had to tell him what to do, but since he hated me, he refused to listen. Kind of like the Tu and Catherine situation, I had to use my friend Deidre as a translator, or a mediator, or both.

"Deidre, can you tell Tommy to touch up the paint on the banisters?"

"Why am I telling him when you're right here?"

"Deidre, just tell him, please. He isn't speaking to me."

"Oh, okay. Um, Tommy, can you touch up the paint on the banisters?" Deidre would say.

"No problem, *Deidre,* I would be glad to." He would look back at me over his shoulder as he responded. I don't know what point he was trying to prove. I still got the banisters painted.

Eventually, Tommy and Corey had a falling-out, so he stopped coming around for good. Corey said it was something about Tommy never giving Corey his change when Tommy would go to the corner store for him. But what I heard happened, because I wasn't at work that day since I always miss the big shit, was that Tommy picked a fight with Corey over some bullshit and Corey called him ungrateful and kicked him out. After that, I never saw Tommy again.

The only reason I could work at the studio was because I was *actually* getting unemployment checks, so when they were about to run out I had to go out and get ANOTHER job. When I told Corey I was leaving, he wasn't happy.

Who else could use Microsoft Word?

"Can't you stay? How much are they paying you?" he asked when I told him about the new job.

"Seventeen dollars an hour."

"Are they hiring?" he asked.

"Not you."

So I had to leave the music studio because, like I've explained, I like eating and living indoors, and I learned an important lesson along the way. If given the option, sleep with the owner instead of the employee. The owner might be broke, too, but at least he has a business and a place to live.

My last day job before I started doing comedy full-time started in March 2014, working in bilingual sales at a stucco supply company. Abbey, my boss, had graduated from my high school, and I think that was one of the reasons I got the job. I actually learned a little Romanian at that job, because Abbey and a majority of the contractors were Romanian, so I had no choice but to learn a little bit. I learned to count from zero to ten. *Ce faci?* (pronounced *Che fetch*), which means "How are you?" and the response, *"Bine,"* which means "good," and the word *"muaca,"* slang for "dumb-dumb." There was more than one occasion where I would mess up something on an order and earn my *"muaca"* for the day.

I didn't know that Romanian was a romance language, similar to Spanish and Italian, until a customer came in and saw my business card on my desk.

"*Dual-che*? Your name is Dual-che? Why you have Romanian name?"

"Wait, what?"

"Dual-che. Is Romanian."

"Okay, we both know I don't have a Romanian name. My name is Dulcé (pronounced dual-say). It's Spanish for sweet."

"Oh, you speak Spanish?"

"Yes, do you?"

"We all speak Spanish. All you have to do is press two."

I laughed so hard I melted into the floor. That man said that to me in 2015 and I still laugh about it. Turns out my name in Romanian is a combination of the Italian and Spanish pronunciation of my name. The "che" from *dolce* and the "dual" from *dulcé*. Who knew?! Also whenever someone calls me Dolce it makes my skin crawl. And thank God for the popularity of the dulcé de leche flavor. One guy I worked with told me that the only reason he knew how to say my name was because that was his favorite flavor of blunt wraps to buy. Classy.

Unlike most bosses, Abbey would never say some slick shit if I yawned at work, like, "Oh, are you tired because you were doing *stand-up* all night?" She was supportive. She let me take off to go to auditions, and she never shamed me for yawning. She DID try to get me to agree to an immigration marriage to a family friend for $5,000 so he could stay in the country. I politely declined because I was going to have to stay married to him for three whole years.

"But it's good money."

"It's not enough money."

"It's five thousand dollars!"

"You don't think I could make five thousand dollars in three years?!"

"Oh. Well . . . hmm. Yeah, you're right."

If anyone was going to be my last boss, I'm glad it was her. She always pushed and supported me. We would have craft days where she helped me get ready for a kid's birthday party I was working. Or she'd "hire" me to make things for her family parties, like cutting out shapes and designs for her stepdaughter's baby shower or making fascinators for her sister's 1920s party. I'm not going to say every day was great, but most days were good. Especially when certain customers came in. There was Overalls, who would bring in big bags of veggies from his garden for Abbey and who taught me a bit about guns, IRS no-knock warrants, and the Dixie Mafia. (Did y'all know there was a Dixie Mafia? I mean just the name is *chef's kiss.* Where is that Netflix documentary? I wanna know everything!) Overalls only hired undocumented workers or parolees so he could control his workforce with threat of jail or deportation *or* his Mafia family. What a guy. He had a cousin who worked for him who was always sunburned. Just a human tomato picking up supplies.

Then there was Doll Eyes. A very sweet man who looked like a tall Gene Wilder, who would come to see me do stand-up.

He even hired me to perform at his company Christmas party at his house. There was Good Ole Boy, and I loved Good Ole Boy. Mind you, I was thirty-two and he had to be about fifty. He was married and had a daughter in college. He didn't come in often, but when he did we were both so happy to see each other. We would talk and flirt and laugh and one day he said, "I need to get out of here. 'Cuz if I wasn't married, you and me would have some fun." Yes, sir, we would have! If that man wasn't married you wouldn't be reading this book. I would have become an upper-middle-class housewife with an SUV, toting the latest Vera Bradley bag, clad in head-to-toe UGA attire because that's my husband's team and I don't even like that team. My children would be adorable wearing all-monogrammed everything. Have I thought about this? A little. But it was never meant to be.

When I worked at the stucco place, I started getting more stand-up and performance work. Eventually I got a manager and was able to leave day jobs for good. I told Abbey that if I made it big I'd get her a Mercedes, because she was so supportive. I am still planning to get her that car, but it has to be a good one. I just have to buy my mom a house first, and then, Abbey—I got you.

DUMB SHIT PEOPLE SAY AT WORK

People talk crazy at all kinds of jobs—corporate jobs, retail jobs, auto body jobs, white collar jobs. And yes, even glamorous comedy TV jobs. This list will run down some of my all-time favorites.

- *"I didn't sit in traffic for this shit."* One of my favorites. I just love hearing people say this. You have to be ornery as hell.

- *"Let's put a pin in it!"* I mean what does this even mean?

- *"Let's table this for another time."* What table? This is an office, not an Applebee's.

- *"Why don't you have kids yet?"* When I was twenty-seven years old, working in an office of about twenty women who all had kids, one lady asked me why I didn't have a kid yet. When I said I wasn't married, she said you don't have to be married to have kids, so my reply was, "Maybe *you* don't have to be married to have kids." My supervisor pulled me out by the shirt to yell at me. She didn't fire me, though!

- *"Are you tired because you did one of your little comedy shows last night?"* There was a woman at one job who would ask this if I yawned even once. Bitch, what? And yes, yes I am.

- *"We need to increase productivity."* Then y'all need to pay more. I am giving ten-dollars-an-hour worth of effort and giving a fuck.

- *"I want to download the situation with you."* I am not a laptop! Do not download anything on me, with me, or anywhere near me.

- *"You don't own this place, you are not Victoria, and you don't know her Secret."* This is actually something that I said to my manager at Victoria's Secret when she was acting like folding G-strings was the Lord's work. I don't think it's dumb at all!

FOUR

Divorce Papers

I experienced my first crush in third grade. Bobby was Black and Korean, and he was cute. That's about all I needed to know at that point in life to fall for a man. We lost touch after third grade, but he recently hit me up on Facebook. He was cute back in grade school, so I thought maybe he'd aged well and we could get married and have babies finally, but when I scrolled through his photos it was a solid *hell no*. Bobby grew up to be a forty-year-old man who was trying to be a rapper, plus he had a wife and multiple children. I looked at his pictures and thought, *What is happening, bro?* I replied in a nice way, like a lady, asking him how he'd been, and then I went on my merry-ass way. How very dare you come back into my life after all these years just to confirm "if we went to elementary school together?" Yes. Yes, we did. He didn't say anything back. I hope he bet someone money that we were in the third grade together and they were like, "Even if you were, she isn't going to respond." But I did. And I hope he won a hundred dollars.

After Bobby, there was Dustin. He was also in my third grade class. He was a white boy from Oklahoma. My father and brother were born in Oklahoma and we used to live there, so I thought that was some kind of connection. BUT he had other horrible qualities, as you'll see.

Before I ever met Dustin, I learned an important life lesson, thanks to my Auntie Hope. She's my mother's ex-sister-in-law, and I remember visiting her house in Coral Springs, Florida, to celebrate my sixth birthday. Auntie Hope let me try my first wine cooler on my sixth or seventh birthday because after all, it was a party. She is very New Orleans. So my cousin Kiki told Auntie Hope that somebody at school called her the N-word, and Auntie Hope gave her some motherly advice about how to handle the situation.

"Kiki, next time you beat them until they forget that word."

And then she took a sip of her peach wine cooler.

As soon as Auntie Hope walked away, my mom pulled me aside.

"Duce. Don't you do that. You will get in trouble and it'll prove them right in their own mind. Say something that's gonna hurt their feelings instead."

I guess that stayed with me. I don't remember why Dustin got mad at me at school one day. Nobody was cheating on each other or stealing credit cards, since we were children. Whatever it was, Dustin went there. He called me the N-word.

Now, I could have beaten him up, if I wanted to. But my mother's words rang in my ears.

"You don't have to hurt them. Say something that's gonna hurt their feelings."

OK, Mommy, I got you! I looked at Dustin and thought, *This boy just said the meanest thing.* That should have been foreshadowing for my life, and for every woman's life. At that moment, I knew I needed something that would make him feel the way he was trying to make me feel. Then I remembered that Dustin had cried in class about his parents getting divorced. Respecting my mom's advice, I stared right into Dustin's beady racist eyes and said, "Yeah? Well, your parents are getting divorced and your dad's gonna marry a Black lady and you're gonna be an N-word, too!"

It worked. Dustin busted out crying. Adults always taught kids to say, "Sticks and stones will break my bones, but words will never hurt me." We ALL knew that was a bold-faced lie, and this was further confirmation. Our teacher, Mrs. Hudson, saw Dustin in tears and called him to her desk to find out what happened.

Dustin repeated what I said and started crying again. Making himself the victim like the little racist he was. Or, more likely, the racists his parents taught him to be.

Mrs. Hudson immediately called me to her desk.

"Dulcé! Why would you say that to Dustin?!"

"Mrs. Hudson, he called me the N-word," I said. She dropped her head, gave a heavy sigh, and told me to go sit down. I almost skipped back to my seat. He was in trouble AND I made him cry. My mom was a genius. Dustin was sent to the office and was gone the rest of the day. When I think about this, thirty years later, I have to look at the significance of this moment. My fifty-something-year-old white teacher at a predominately white school in an affluent suburb of Atlanta believed *me*. She took my side, and Dustin was punished. There are still Black children all over the country that are being harassed and disrespected by other students and teachers, and nothing is being done. I do hope Dustin's dad didn't marry a Black woman. Sis don't need them problems.

My crush *did* end there. I might have been in the third grade, but I knew not to let a male human talk to me crazy. Years later, I was telling the story of Dustin to a group of comedians on the back ramp of the Relapse Theater in Atlanta. I was around two years in as a comic, so I was still doing small shows and open mic nights. Eddie Ifft was headlining at the Laughing Skull that weekend and he heard me tell the story about Dustin. The next day the manager of the club called me and said that Eddie Ifft liked the story and wanted me to come feature for him on his last Sunday show. This was my first feature spot and my mom's advice helped me get it. My mom's guidance is how I became a stand-up comic from age five and on.

Between Dustin and my actual engagement to Jamal (more on him soon), there were a few boys, but none stuck. There was Junior in Atlanta, who was friends with my brother. This was in 1995, about the time I started to learn that dudes might have crushes, but they wouldn't want people to know because I was the fat girl. Junior liked me, but he kept it quiet. When I was twelve years old he was my first kiss. He was staying over one night with Lawrence, and he got off the bunk bed, walked over, and kissed me. I lost my virginity to him four years later when he came to my house one day after school. My brother was still at school and my mom was still at work. I found out years later that most teen pregnancies occur between three p.m. to five p.m. Makes total sense. I told Junior about losing my virginity to him a few years ago, and he said, "Nah, that ain't true. I can't be that important." What a sweetheart.

Then, in the eighth grade, there was Josué, who was from El Salvador. He was the first boy to openly like me, but he still didn't want everybody to know. That boy tried so hard to have sex with me, which was wild because we were both thirteen. Like, dude, gross. I still got dolls for Christmas! He wanted to retire at twenty-five years old. That was his goal. And I wanted to believe in him. I really did. But all I could say to him was, "How are you going to do that? You are currently flunking out of high school." He told me not to worry about it, which meant he either had no plan, OR . . . drugs. Thankfully he later just dropped out of high school and started working construction with his dad and uncles. Josué was a ding-dong, but eventually I focused my attention on high school theater and Miguel.

Miguel was my biggest crush in high school. He was Mexican, and he was sweet, smart, and funny. Everybody had a crush on him. I was so starry-eyed over this guy, if Miguel didn't know I had a crush on him, he was a solid-gold fool. All of our friends and his sister knew. One day my mom came to pick me up from school and I guess she'd been calling my name for a while before I actually heard her.

"Duce, you couldn't hear me because you were staring at that boy," she told me when I finally came out of my trance. "You had stars in your eyes."

Miguel was a boy who could be trusted. Even my mom trusted him, and she only met him that one time. She thought every other boy was going to take advantage of me. Miguel was protective of me, though, so I felt safe. My mom let me go to a hotel party at a Red Roof Inn once because I told her Miguel was going to be there. I got to this hotel party, though, and I looked around and noticed it was me and about five boys who were all drinking. I knew all of them, but I got a bad feeling. I looked at the numbers and was like, nah, I'm gonna wind up on the news, I'm good.

So I decided to call my mom to pick me up. I do not like marijuana and I'm not a huge drinker, so back then I would have had more fun memorizing lines for a scene from *Buffy the Vampire Slayer*. The Red Roof Inn was not worth getting murdered over, and Miguel wasn't there, so I called my mom to pick me up. She was very confused.

"Why'd you call me so soon? You were only gone an hour."

"They were all high and drunk. Miguel wasn't there, and one of them was too big to fight."

"Well, then I'm glad you called. We don't need any problems."

There were other high school boys besides Miguel. My first high school boyfriend didn't even go to my school. We met at the Georgia Academic Decathlon. It was basically the Nerd Olympics. I was in gifted classes, but this was too much. Why would I spend my free time being tested about the folk music of the Andes, or math with nothing but letters in it? Ridiculous. His name was Ian and he lived two hours away in a small town near the Alabama state line. He was nice enough. We talked on the phone, he took me to prom (missing his to do so), and he got me a silver ring with a blue stone for a Christmas present because that is what I asked for. I still have it, actually.

We broke up after he was rude to me, when my mom and I drove two hours to go to his graduation. Me and Ian were down in his den hanging out, and he wanted to get . . . a little frisky. I said no because my mother and his whole family were upstairs. He started talking to me crazy, and then he threatened me. That was the day that I learned that if a man is rude, I should tell my mom so we can handle it. I marched upstairs to tell my mom AND his mom. His mother was livid. She called him into the kitchen, and I stood there while the moms ripped him a new one.

In college I didn't date much. I was at an all-women's school. I didn't have a lot of money to go out all the time, and the theater department kept us very busy. Not to mention schoolwork and on-campus activities. I mean, I can blame it on all those things, but going to a women's college was obviously the main reason. Plus, I did not want to get pregnant in college. I had plans for my future. I wanted to have a steady job and a husband who *also* had a steady job BEFORE I had kids. Fast-forward to now, when I wake up every day wondering where this man is. I have the job, so this man is late.

I used to work second shift at the Gwinnett County medical records office in Lawrenceville, Georgia. There is nothing that will fuck up your social life more than working from three p.m. to eleven p.m. merging and deleting duplicate medical records. It was a special project the county was doing, and the white lady running it wanted to work those hours, so I spent six weeks of my life not being able to do anything except go to Applebee's at 11:05 p.m. At this job, I met a very thin man named Jamal. One night after our shift, Jamal invited me to dinner, so as soon as eleven p.m. hit we sprinted to the car and sped to Applebee's so we could eat before the stroke of midnight. He was very sweet to me, and what you need to know about this relationship was that we started dating in November 2005, and he proposed to me three months later on Valentine's Day 2006. I ended the engagement in March and broke up with him for good in April. It was a whirlwind, and not the kind you want to be swept up in.

His good qualities were that he was sweet and he wanted to marry me, but he was twenty-six years old, had a car I wasn't sure he could pay for, and one day he told me he had never been to the dentist. His teeth and breath were fine. Relax. I also remember we were walking up a hill one day and he seemed to be walking a little bit unevenly, so I asked him what that was all about.

"I have scoliosis that was never treated. My legs are different sizes."

"Cool. Cool, cool, cool."

I am not trying to say this man looked like Quasimodo, who rang the bell and scared all the townspeople in *The Hunchback of Notre Dame*. On flat ground, you couldn't even tell the difference. He was actually a handsome man, and he did love me. My mother was not convinced that he was the one for me, though. My mom said that if I came home with ugly grandkids, she was not fucking with them.

"I'll put hats on them and send them back," she told me.

She also told me to look at some of Jamal's family photo albums, to see how my genes might interact with his genes. I told my husband-to-be that I wanted to see photos of his aunties and grandparents, just because I loved him so much and wanted to know everything I could about who he came from. Really I was trying to see how our genes would mix. As I flipped through the photos, I started to worry. I come from pretty people, but I did not know if my ancestors were strong enough for the battle ahead. If I got into this gene pool, I was sure to drown.

I am not trying to sound hateful. His gene pool was NOT why I broke off the engagement with this man. When he proposed on Valentine's Day, by getting down on one knee in his bedroom, I was so happy. I hadn't seen the family photos yet, and I also did not know about his family's crazy-ass legal troubles. I said yes, and told my mom. Her response was, "Duce. Are you sure?"

"Yes ma'am, he's so nice. And he loves me. And he's proud to be with me."

I think I got caught up in being young, wanting to have a family, and going to five weddings my senior year of college. But then I found out about all the debt he had. He'd filed for bankruptcy because his father told him to keep taking student loan money from the government after he had dropped out of school. Miss Sallie Mae or Mr. Freddie Mac found out and wanted their money back. He of course didn't have it. That's why he got the loans in the first place! It's really messed up when you think about it. He also lived at home with his parents because he couldn't get his own place with a fresh new bankruptcy on his credit report. I lived at home, too, because I had graduated from college six months before. So where were we going to sleep? His parents' house? How could I live that way?

His mom didn't even like me being in her kitchen, so what was I going to do? Stand outside the kitchen as a married woman and beg my mother-in-law to hand me some salt? If the living situation wasn't enough of a red flag, my friends started warning me about this man's debt becoming my debt when we got married, and finally it sank in. I didn't have any negative credit history, or any credit history at all really. My record was clean and I was not looking to get married and then have to pay back a bunch of money I didn't owe. So that March, I tried to give him the quarter-karat ring back.

"We haven't known each other that long, and this is moving too fast," I told him. I didn't mention the debt, or the family photos. "Let's just date some more. I still love you."

He wasn't too happy, but he told me to keep the ring, and we did date for another month. During that time there was one night I made Jamal wear two condoms at once, because he had "joked" about getting me pregnant and trapping me. The final straw was that he started getting angry if another man talked to me. No, sir. I have seen enough Lifetime movies to know how that goes. So I broke up with him for good in April. I gave him the ring back in front of my house with my mom ready as backup if there were any issues. I was sad. Not like *sad* sad. And definitely not sad enough to bind my life to a messy situation where I'd be broke with ugly children whose own grandmother wanted to cover them up with hats.

So for a few months, I just worked and pursued acting. I got a job at an auto body shop, and I basically ended up managing the place. That's how I met The Mechanic.

I was always on the phone with this guy named Ray at a nearby car dealership, ordering parts and flirting on the phone. When I finally met this boy in person we looked at each other and were like, nah, but he did say that I should meet his roommate. At the time I had a turquoise 1992 Pontiac Grand Am with 286,000 miles on it that was leaking oil and transmission fluid. But like a slow leak. A classy leak. One day it started cutting off when I tried to make a turn, especially a right, so I decided to take it to the dealership. As soon as I rolled into the bay at the dealership it cut out again, so I jumped out and yelled, "Somebody come fix this car! It's *dangerous*." I knew all the service writers so I knew they would give me a good deal. But they insisted that this one specific guy had to be the one to fix it. I didn't care, as long as someone could stop my car cutting off in the middle of Atlanta traffic.

I see this short man walking toward me, and something told me, "You are going to know this man for a very long time." I had no idea what that meant, but I believed it. This guy was the roommate Ray kept telling me about. He was extremely cocky, and I knew that by his walk. I don't usually go for cocky because it has a tendency to become rude very quickly, but he was cute. I found out later that since the day Ray came to my office four months before, he had been talking me up to The Mechanic. He was about my height and my complexion. He had locs that went past his shoulders that were dyed honey blond on the ends. He had on a baseball cap, glasses, and behind the glasses he had brown eyes. A shade of brown I have never seen before or since. What really stood out to me were his hands and his arms. I love a man with strong hands and arms.

He walked right up and asked why my car had so much mileage on it.

"Why? What do you do with your car besides drive it?" I said. "Do you flatbed it everywhere? It's a car. I drive it."

I think he liked that, because he said, "My roommate Ray's been telling me about you. Where do you live?"

"Why do you want to know that?" I said.

"I'll take you home."

"Take me home? What if you kill me?"

"Oh, please, I wouldn't kill you. Everybody knows where I work."

"What does that mean?"

"It means get your coat."

I told him my address, and he said his house was down the street from my mom's house, where I was living. He lived two miles from me and worked one mile from me. It was a wonder we had never met before. My mom was still very protective of me, so I called to tell her I was getting a ride home from the dealership.

"Duce, you don't know this man."

"Mommy, he works here. Everyone will see us leave together,

so if I get murdered everyone will know he did it. I'm fine."

That did not convince her, so I put The Mechanic on the phone.

"Can you tell my mom you're not going to murder me?" I said. He looked confused, but he put the phone to his ear and did as I said.

"I'm not going to murder your daughter?"

He didn't sound that convincing, but I could tell this man liked me.

For our first date, in January of 2007, which would also turn out to be our last—even though we kept hanging out for EIGHT YEARS—he was going to take me to dinner and a movie at Buckhead Fork and Screen. I told that man to get the movie tickets ahead of time, but he didn't listen, so when we got to the theater it was sold out. He told me he saw his ex-girlfriend in the crowd, even though I never saw her. I was like, that's a fun omen. That omen manifested three years later when I did meet that ex-girlfriend on a movie set. So, we watched *Talladega Nights* on the screen in his steering wheel, and he took me to Applebee's.

Me and The Mechanic were on and off for almost a decade. I used to do this thing I called "Frankensteining men," where I'd see different men for different reasons, and together they made one man. So I saw The Mechanic for the hang, since he lived right around the corner and he didn't like to go anywhere. I'd go on platonic dates with my homeboy, and then UPS guy for the good sexy time.

UPS guy was tall with medium-brown skin. He was slim and had perfect lips. His voice wasn't deep per se, but it had a weight and authority to it that made you want to do what he said, but with a sarcasm in it that made you want to defy him. I was waiting in line and I met him as he was leaving work, and the store was about to close. I was joking with some people about the long line, and he asked if I needed some help.

"How can you help me? Do you even work here?"

"Yes, I do."

"Why aren't you dressed like you work here? You have on gray sweats."

"I work in the back, so I don't have to wear the uniform."

"Nigga what?"

"How about you let me take you out and I will explain it to you later?"

"I don't know about that. And what about my package?"

"Come use the postage machine and give me your number."

Strangers in line pressured me to give him my number.

"He cute. . . ."

"All right, fine. Here."

"See, that wasn't so hard. I'll hit you up later."

Then I spent the next eight years going back and forth with him.

That day was the last time he worked a day shift. To this very day he still works third shift. So our relationship adapted to his schedule. In a weird twist of fate, his apartment was two doors down from my job at an oncology practice (I told you I had a lot of jobs). I knew Atlanta was small, but damn. I got off work at five p.m. and he had to leave for work at seven p.m., so that gave us a two-hour window to see each other. The first and second time I went to his house I refused to go inside, mainly because I was worried about what would happen if I went inside. I wanted him to take me out, and I knew if I gave up the goodies too quickly, that would be out the window. But the third time I went inside because, well, it was my third time and I ran out of excuses and he said, "Girl, come on," in such a way that I had to go in. Also I had to pee, so it was a win-win. But I made it very clear that I wasn't going in the bedroom and we were just going to talk and watch TV. Talking and watching TV turned into a back rub, which turned into kissing. And it stayed at kissing. Just good, wholesome, above-the-clothes making out and caressing. So I was very confused when I left and was standing outside the door saying to myself, "I feel like I just had sex. I know I didn't have sex because my clothes never came off. What did he do to me? Oh, this man is finna be a problem."

I told my homegirl what happened.

"And you didn't take your clothes off?"

"No!"

"No nip slip or nothing?"

"No, ma'am."

"Oh, girl, he's gonna be a problem."

"GIRL!"

When we finally did hook up I think it was my fifth time going to see him. It was around three a.m. We were talking and then making out and then clothes started to come off, but we both kept saying, "We aren't having sex, we're just . . . getting comfortable." More clothes come off, more making out, now we are in the bedroom. "We aren't having sex . . . the bed is just more comfortable." Now in the bed, there are no more clothes, I'm on top of him. "We aren't having sex, just . . . kissing and rubbing." He puts on a condom. "We aren't having sex, just . . . being careful." More making out and then it happens. And then I say, "Okay, I think we might be having sex."

"Yeah, I think we might be."

It was after that we realized that because of his work schedule, this would be the only arrangement we could have. I loved hooking up with him. For one, he always made me have a catch-up talk before we had sex. There was one night I came over and I was tired from work and doing shows and I told him I just wanted to have sex and go to sleep. He said, "No. We are friends. You are going to sit down and tell me about your day. How was the audition you had?" I was annoyed, but I appreciated it. A month could have gone by and he would ask me about an audition or jewelry event or anything I had going on in my life. He was also the first guy who would touch my whole body when we had sex. I had started to realize that some guys would avoid touching my stomach or my sides, but not this man. He would hug and squeeze my love handles and pinch my cheeks.

Whenever I would get self-conscious, say stop or try to cover up, he would say, "No. I like your body," and then kiss wherever I was trying to cover.

He will never understand how much that helped me change the way I saw myself. Now, he did come with his own nonsense. Asking me to be his mistress but he wasn't married? I had to explain to him that side chicks and mistresses are paid for their silence. Thems the rules, sir. We talked about dating once or twice, but we decided that we didn't want to mess up what we had. He got married a year after I moved away. I do wonder what it would be like if we ever did date. In the long run it would have never worked because he didn't want any more children (oh, yeah, he had kids!), and I wanted to have some kids of my own. We still talk sometimes. He is the only man from my past who calls to check on me and/or tells me how proud he is and he knew I was always going to make it. He also says he is mad at me for leaving, and tells me how much he loved me and all of that. I never know what to feel when he does it because neither one of us can go back in time to fix it, and there is nothing that can happen now. I do love him and have love for him, but he is in a different place. I always think it's interesting how men always say that women can't have sex without emotion and we always get attached. For most of my life it seems to be the opposite.

I hung out with The Mechanic the most because, well, that's where I was the most emotionally invested. All we did was hang out at his house, watch Will Ferrell movies, eat trash food, and fool around. One reason I excused him for never taking me out was that we met during a recession, so I knew how much he was making, or wasn't making. I couldn't ask him to take me to dinner when he was having a hard time paying his mortgage. That's what I told myself at the time. Now I look back and realize that self-worth is pretty valuable. But when you convince yourself that most men don't want you, you live in place of scarcity. I spent too much time with that man, but I just liked talking to him.

Another thing that took me a while to realize was the fact he only really wanted to see me during the cold months. There's a pattern in my life where men hang with me during winter, and then when the sun comes out, they disappear. It's called cuffing season. And I am a cuffing season All-Star! The Mechanic did this *for years*. Where did they go? Who knows, but the first fall day that dropped below seventy-five degrees, there they were, asking me to hang. The Mechanic only acted right from Labor Day to St. Patty's Day. The rest of the year he could have been out on a pontoon boat with four redneck strippers, but he wasn't, because he rarely left his house.

Now, I liked talking to The Mechanic, but I also liked that he was a grown man with a job, his own home that he OWNED, and two cars. The Rules says that when you meet a man like that, YOU TRAP HIS ASS, SIS. His house was a split-level, and I hate split-level homes. They are maddening, but still. It was *his*. After my engagement and worrying that I'd end up living in a house with a country-ass mother-in-law who wouldn't let me boil water in the kitchen, I was like—jackpot. I am trapping this man the best I can. I was cooking for The Mechanic and giving him the best blowjobs of his life. In return he was quoting lines from *Talladega Nights*, fixing my car, and NOT taking me out to dinner. So I served him some papers.

This was about the time that Britney Spears and Kevin Federline were splitting up, so I think I was inspired by their divorce that was on the news every hour on the hour. I had only been hanging out with The Mechanic for a few months and there was definitely no talk of marriage or babies coming out of that man's mouth, but I got fed up with him disappearing for days and then texting me to hang out. He was playing with my emotions, so I decided to divorce his ass, sort of. I kept telling him I was going to divorce him and he wouldn't believe me. So in the words of one of my favorite Southern Black proverbs, "I can show you better than I can tell you."

Now I am a BEAST with Microsoft Word, so I sat down and designed some divorce papers that looked real as hell. I did some Google searches to find out what divorce papers actually look like, wrote them up, put them in a little folder, and drove to his job to serve his ass.

"What's this?" he asked when I handed him the manila envelope.

"You've been served," I said in my most official *Law & Order* I-am-not-fucking-around tone of voice.

He looked at the papers, a little confused, and then we both started laughing.

"Are you trying to get rid of me?"

"You're already gone, sir! I want those papers signed in triplicate!"

"I am never signing these," he said.

"You'll be hearing from my lawyer." And I pulled off. I immediately called my homegirl and we laughed about it on my drive home.

I wish I could tell you I sped away and left that man's life for good, but you know that's not true. You saw the name of the chapter. Those divorce papers became a running joke between us for years. Any time he'd make me mad, I'd tell him to sign the papers, and he'd refuse. He told me recently that he still has those papers in his memory box somewhere, so either he did really love me, or he's a hoarder who keeps mementos from the women whose hearts he's broken.

The Mechanic owned his own home, and that home happened to be his own personal Dave & Buster's. He had a huge TV and video games, poker and pool tables, and darts. He smoked weed, and I hated and still hate the smell of weed. I remember one day he was smoking out of a bowl that looked exactly like a dick and two balls. I don't think he had any clue, so I told him.

"Bro, that bowl looks like a dick and balls."

"What? No, it doesn't."

"I'm just telling you it looks like a dick. I have seen other bowls and they do not look like a man's dick."

The Mechanic was homophobic, so I never saw him smoke

out of that bowl again. He also loved watching MMA, which I did not like to watch. It's violent, and the fighters are ugly and always bleeding. Give me a good ole American Professional Wrestling match any day. Knowing his homophobic tendencies, I casually commented that MMA, where two grown men in tiny tight shorts wrap their legs around each other's heads, is homoerotic. I know it's not, but I did not want to watch MMA. So if that meant using his own ignorance and prejudice against him, then so be it.

"What're you talking about? No, it's not."

"I'm just saying you did that to me last night. He's all up in that man. And that guy has Condom Depot written across his ass. Come on."

My plan worked. He changed the channel.

One night when I was hanging out at Dave & Buster's/The Mechanic's, I was feeling tired of his on-and-off attention. He had some friends over to play poker, and in walks this gorgeous man—The Dummy. I had met The Dummy a few times, but that night, he looked GOOD. He had always been walking sex but this was on another level. I was watching these fools waste money playing poker. I cannot stand gambling, it's the biggest waste of money known to man besides insurance. (I mean really. If I don't file a claim, refund my premium.) If you want to lose two or three dollars on the lotto, fine, but putting down two hundred dollars that should go toward your light bill on a poker game? I don't get it. I was getting bored, and I wanted to entertain myself, *and* I didn't think that The Mechanic actually cared that much about me based on the way he was treating me. The Dummy kept winning hands and I said it was all thanks to me, so I put myself in the pot.

"Whoever wins this game wins a date with me," I said.

I saw The Mechanic's eyes light the fuck up, like he was mad, but he would never admit that. He'd told me plenty of times that he didn't want me to be his girlfriend, he just wanted me to be around. Okay. That's fine. So we aren't together. I put myself in that pot. And The Dummy won! And The Mechanic tried to hide that he wasn't happy.

We exchanged numbers. Even though I owed The Mechanic nothing, I told The Dummy that I would only go on a date with him if The Mechanic was cool with it. The Dummy talked to The Mechanic and then told me everything was cool, but later I found out that their conversation went like this:

Dummy: What's up with you and Dulcé?

The Mechanic: I guess nothing.

And that's what he took to mean, "I give you my blessing to take Dulcé out."

So The Dummy and I started dating. The conversations weren't great, but sex with that man was amazing. It was like someone had taken my body and made a mold that would perfectly fit his body. The first time we had sex, we both looked at each other like, "Oh, no. This is too good." We couldn't get through a movie or a conversation without jumping on top of each other.

He wasn't that bright, which meant the sex was good. Because we all know that dumb, country, or broke men have the best dick. He was the first man to ever make me breakfast. It was so exciting, but the minute he started tap-tap-tapping those eggs, I knew there was trouble.

I was lying in his bed that morning, just minding my business, when I heard the *tap-tap-tap* of someone tapping metal on the sink in the kitchen.

"What are you doing, babe?" I asked.

"Making you breakfast."

Tap-tap-tap.

"Oh, okay."

Tap-tap-tap.

Hearing a man make you eggs should be relaxing, like you're being treated like the queen you deserve to be treated as. Instead . . .

Tap-tap-tap.

"That's a lot of shells," I whispered to myself as I got out of bed and got dressed. "I should go in there."

The tapping was starting to unnerve me, and something was telling me NOT to go in there, to just sit my ass down and wait until he delivered an omelet platter to me, with a rose and some hot sauce on the side.

Tap-tap-tap.

That was it. I had to find out what this man was doing to those eggs.

"Babe? What's going on in here?"

Tap-tap-tap.

"I'm trying to get the sperm out."

"What? What sperm?"

"My mom told me this right here is the sperm, so I have to get it out."

His mother had led this poor man to believe that the little white ball of protein inside a raw egg was semen.

"That's not sperm."

"For real?"

"Yes, for real. Sperm just doesn't 'hang out' in an egg."

I had to kiss him to erase what just happened from my brain. It didn't work. At least the sex was good. So was the breakfast.

The Dummy and I didn't last long, and not because he thought making eggs involved extracting chicken semen from an egg. The man spent his rent money on a pair of expensive, fur-lined roller skates with Oscar the Grouch and Big Bird painted on the sides. Sex is good, but no sex is good enough to tolerate that bullshit. I also should mention that before I came along, The Dummy lived with The Mechanic, and these skates were the reason The Mechanic kicked The Dummy out. Now, I know I may not have presented enough evidence for this young man to earn the nickname of "The Dummy." Well, ladies and gentlemen of the jury, please allow me to present my most damning piece of evidence. One night after a couple rounds of the sexy time, The Dummy told me that he really liked me and was attracted to me, but one of the reasons he was dating me was to get back at The Mechanic, because a girl he was dating chose The Mechanic over him. He told me the whole story.

So, The Mechanic got The Dummy a job detailing cars at another dealership, and this girl, we'll call her Makeup, was working in the front office. The Dummy and Makeup start hanging out, and one day he brings Makeup down to the dealership where The Mechanic works, and they get cool. Now at this time The Dummy was renting a room from The Mechanic, and Makeup would come over to the house and stay the night with The Dummy because they were dating. So one day Makeup goes down to the dealership where The Mechanic works to say hi or whatever, and the folks at the dealership tell her that The Mechanic is home sick. Well, for some reason she has this man's phone number. She calls him, brings over some soup and juice, and now she is moved on up to the room of the owner of the house! Leaving The Dummy in his feelings, mad that now she is coming over to the house to see The Mechanic and apparently using me for his revenge. The story is amazing, but he is an idiot.

And then he nodded off with a lit Newport in his hand. I had to wake him up to make sure he didn't kill us and his roommate. I was stunned. One, the fact he was dumb enough to tell me this, and two, that he fell asleep right after like I wasn't going to say anything. Now here comes the Tea!

On my first date with The Mechanic he randomly mentioned that his ex-girlfriend was there. That was Makeup! And if you can't figure out why I am calling her that—she wore too much makeup. It was either that or Forehead. I'm being nice.

Makeup and I were extras on a movie, and we had been waiting to go on set for five hours. After that amount of time, small talk goes out the window and the little circle of friends you have made is talking about real shit. We are talking about significant others, and Makeup pulls out the business card of her current boyfriend. He is also an actor, so his photo is on the card.

"Girl," I said. "I used to hook up with him when we worked on a play together a few years before."

"No way! Y'all still friends?"

"No, he never told me he had a girlfriend," I said.

The next thing I know, she's handing me her phone.

"Who is this?" I asked.

"It's him. Say hi."

Oh, they want to play games.

I got on the phone and cursed him out. Ended that call and then cursed *her* out for being rude and petty. Bitch, what.

We finally got called to set, and she asked who I was seeing, so I started telling her about The Mechanic. I never said the man's name, just talked about our relationship.

She says, "Wait. Is he the only Black guy that works at *redacted name* dealership? You mean *The Mechanic's real name*?"

We both start yelling and jumping up and down. And a disembodied A.D. (Assistant Director) yells, "Quiet on set!"

The first thing she says is, "Oh. My. God. He is the most selfish person I have ever met. You know he never came to see a single show I've been in?"

"Oh my goodness. Me neither. I thought it was me, but it's him."

"Wait a minute. I saw him on a date with a girl at Buckhead Fork & Screen. That was you?"

"Yes! Oh my God."

"How was the date?"

"It sucked. He didn't buy the tickets in advance like I told him to, and we ended up watching a movie in his car and going to Applebee's!"

"Dummy."

"This is just a shot in the dark, but since we are two for two, let's go for the third. Are you the girl that started dating *Dummy's real name* and then started dating *The Mechanic's real name*?"

"Yes! How do you know about that?"

"Because The Dummy is so cocky and stupid that he told me that he was dating me to get back at The Mechanic for dating you."

"The Dummy is hot and the sex is ah-mazing!"

"A-fucking-mazing. You can't function."

"But there is just something about The Mechanic."

So we keep talking about the various characteristics about these boys, but I can't shake the feeling that I have known her from somewhere. Well, turns out she went to my high school and we had met a few times in passing. Atlanta is too small. So this is when things start to get ridiculous.

Then Makeup suggests, "Hey, let's take a picture."

We take a selfie.

"Now let's send it to The Mechanic? Or I can put it on Facebook and tag us and him."

"Ahhh, girl. We don't need to do that." It was highly unnecessary.

I have no idea why she and The Mechanic broke up, and honestly, I don't think I cared. But this was some triflin'-ass nonsense.

"What? But why? Ugh, fine."

Now at this point we had exchanged numbers and she found out I was doing a play at Ansley Park Playhouse called *A Sunday Afternoon at Loehmann's*. Apparently I booked the role she had auditioned for and she wanted to come see the show. I told her I would give her one of my comp tickets. We joked about her inviting The Mechanic to the show because he never came to any of our plays. She messaged me that she was coming and that she ASKED The Mechanic to come with her, but he said he had to take care of his grandpa, so he couldn't make it.

I was furious. What kind of messy bullshit was this? So I tell her that was rude and inappropriate, and she messages me back, "Oh, it's fine," and to "Get over it." So I called the theater and canceled her comp ticket. You want to talk shit, ma'am, then you have to pay full price. The Mechanic knew that I had met her, because he texted me the day after with a very appropriate, "What the hell! How did this happen?" I explained the movie set, and he said, "Makes sense." What was highly inappropriate was her inviting him to my show. I called him to get this sorted out because . . . I was still seeing him.

"Okay, so you know asking you to come to my show wasn't my idea?"

"Yeah, it sounds like some shit she would do. I can't make it anyway. I gotta help my grandpa."

"I know, she told me. Just wanted to make sure you knew I wasn't involved."

"You good."

I leave and go to the theater to get ready for my show and go to the box office to make sure this messy heifer does not get a comp ticket. They say she is off the list. I'm happy. I head to my dressing room to get ready. As the show starts, I see her run in as the lights come up. The crowd was very light that night. Maybe twenty people in a hundred-seat house, and she has on a lime-green sweater. Can't miss her. At the end of the show she meets me in the lobby.

"Thank you again for the comp. Twenty-five dollars for a ticket is high."

What? She wasn't supposed to get a comp.

"The Mechanic was here, but he had to leave early. It's so nice that they cast you for this role. It's an interesting choice."

"He wasn't here." I had to focus on that because I know she was upset about not booking the role.

"Yeah he was, you just missed him."

"He wasn't here. I saw when you came in. You sat house left and you were alone. I don't know what you are lying for, but I don't have time for this."

"Oh, it was a joke. You need to relax."

"It wasn't funny and I don't play like that. And I canceled your comp ticket, so I don't know how you got one. Have a nice night."

I walked straight to the box office to find out how that damn girl got a comp ticket. Apparently she was running in just as the show started and said, "Comp ticket," and they let her in without checking because the show was starting. I called The Mechanic to tell him about her claiming he came to the show, and he said, "Yeah, she keeps shit going."

I blocked her number that day. But, Makeup, if you're reading this book, I just want you to know that The Mechanic did come to see me in that play. Was I dating someone else at the time and it was the final week of the show even though I had been in it for almost a year? Yes. But that's not the point. He said he was going to come, and he did. In the end, that's what we wanted. For him to come see *me* in that show.

Eventually, after another breakup, I made my way back to The Mechanic, like I always did. I remember one day asking him straight out if he loved me. He never said it, so I wanted to know.

When I asked, he gave me a thumbs-up.

In the eight years we went back and forth, he said it less than five times. I wouldn't say it because he wouldn't say it. I came to realize we had an emotionally abusive relationship. I told him that and his response was, "I never hit you," so, yeah, that was healthy.

I was Frankensteining men, so I had to make sure I was being responsible. No man had ever, um, what's the best way to put it . . . I never had sex without a condom from ages eighteen to thirty-six years of age, and to this day no man has ever shot the club up, if you know what I mean. I am saving that for marriage. But accidents happen. That's how most of us got here. I used to tell doctors that my birth control methods were condoms and prayer. Most doctors didn't laugh, but a few did. When I did try to get on birth control, doctors would always convince me not to go on anything—the pill, an IUD, a NuvaRing. One doctor, who did laugh at my condoms-and-prayer bit, said, "Do you always use condoms?" I said yes, sir. "And you're thirty?" Yes. "You're good. You know what you're doing."

And that was it. Another time I tried to get birth control, and this was through the Grady Health System in Atlanta. If you had a Grady card you basically had free access to an argument with a medical professional. When I asked for some sort of birth control, the doctor didn't waste time.

"No."

"Excuse me, Dr. Patel?"

"We're worried about your weight. I can't give you birth control."

"You know what will make me gain a lot of weight? A baby. Plus-size women can take birth control."

"Well, it says you smoke cigarettes. That is very dangerous with birth control pills."

"I can quit. What about a patch?"

"No."

"A shot?"

"No, ma'am."

"A chastity belt, put a rubber band around my knees, self-esteem. Help me, bitch."

She offered me a pelvic exam, and since I was already there I said yes. As I lay on the exam table, there was a NuvaRing display, like a beacon of hope!

"What about a NuvaRing?"

"No, ma'am."

"WHY NOT?!"

"Oh, no, ma'am. You can't have the NuvaRing. Black women don't like to put the hand in the vagina."

What the fuck! This racist bitch! But then I thought about it. Damn it, she was right. I don't like to put the hand in the vagina. I hate tampons.

"What if I put the NuvaRing on the man's penis? We do it like a ring toss situation and then he puts it in?"

I thought it was a cunning plan, but maybe I was spending too much time with The Dummy.

"It doesn't work that way."

So I left with nothing, except condoms and prayer.

My experiences with doctors have not been the best. I never had a pregnancy scare (thank you, Jesus) but I do pay very close attention to my menstrual cycle. Once, after hooking up with The Mechanic, or as I liked to call it "paying for an oil change," I got my full-on period twice in the same month. I told this to The Mechanic, and he very confidently said, "Maybe I just hit something."

I needed a professional opinion, because that man had lost his mind, so I got myself to the DeKalb Women's Medical Center to find out the real medical reason I was bleeding, because I knew it wasn't that The Mechanic's dick had "hit something." It was big, but it wasn't debilitating.

I was very worried when I came in, but the nurses were ready to help. They did various exams and took a sonogram. I met with a doctor who was sitting behind a giant mahogany desk. A slender white man with short brown hair. Mid-forties, slightly hunched over. Framed medical degrees hung on the wall behind him. This man had more degrees than a thermometer. He was a damn scholar. I felt reassured that he could give me an answer, because all the degrees on his wall were telling me that he was well-educated in the Gynecological Arts. He opens my file. He starts reading. "Condoms and prayer. Hmm. Funny." And then finds the sonogram. He looks over it. He looks up at me, and back at the sonogram. He puts down the file, very serious, and looks up at me, straight into my eyes.

"Well, Ms. Sloan."

"Yes? What is it, Dr. Lang?"

"He probably just hit something."

"Excuse me? You're a medical doctor and you just told me the same thing a MECHANIC told me. I know there are a lot of tubes and hoses, but it's not the same thing!"

"I'm sorry. A mechanic did what?"

"Are those degrees behind you even real? You cannot be serious? What did he hit?"

"Who knows for sure."

"YOU KNOW!"

"Ms. Sloan, it will be fine."

I wanted to flip this man's desk, but it was pure mahogany.

"I am not paying my co-pay."

"Now, Ms. Sloan . . . "

"What will you do, arrest me?"

I did end up paying my twenty-five-dollar co-pay, because it turns out they can arrest you or maybe just fine you. But let's just say I am no longer allowed at the DeKalb Women's Medical Center.

Of course as soon as I stepped outside that building I called The Mechanic.

"Hello?"

"GUESS WHAT."

"What."

"So I'm at the gyno and the doctor said, and I quote,

'He probably just hit something.'"

"No, he didn't," he said, laughing.

"Yes, he did. And when I asked what in there you could have hit he said, 'Who knows for sure?'"

"Shouldn't he know?" Laughing more.

"Bro! I said I been here all morning for you to tell me the same thing a mechanic told me!"

Laughing uncontrollably.

"And you still had to pay that co-pay?"

"I almost flipped the motherfucker's desk. They told me I can't come back."

"Don't get arrested." Still laughing. I'm pretty sure I can hear him crying.

"This is all your fault. I hate you."

"Okay, call me later. I'm glad I didn't break you." Laughing more.

"GET OFF MY PHONE! I'll call you later."

I was furious, and The Mechanic was very proud. He laughed for DAYS. Maybe even years.

We went on seeing each other for so long that every time I brought this man up to my friends, they would say, "Stop talking to me about him. I don't want to hear it." As toxic as our relationship could be, with him only coming around in the cold months and saying "I love you" with a double thumbs-up, I loved this dude. In 2010 he went to Afghanistan for a year to work as a mechanic at a base, and I was so nervous. I sent him a care package. I had a Dell phone with a big-ass screen, and I loved that thing. I'd Google Chat with The Mechanic all the time, even with the wild-ass time difference. I'd lost my job while he was gone, so I reminded him of our divorce and asked him for my alimony, and reminded him how dangerous my car was and how much work it needed. He actually did send me four hundred dollars, even though I was expecting eight hundred. We kept on this way for the whole year he was gone. I could not even quit this man when I was in Atlanta and he was in Central Asia, because he asked me to wait for him before he left. I was talking to him one day and our connection dropped. I couldn't get in touch with him for almost two days, and when he was finally back on, he sent me a message explaining his absence that simply said, "Rocket attack."

What the fuck was wrong with this man? I thought he was dead. You can't just text "Rocket attack." When he did get back to Atlanta, he waited a full month to tell me he was back. When I finally saw him, he gave me a CZ-and-onyx tennis bracelet, and when I asked him what was going to happen with our relationship, since I waited for him, he said he didn't want to be with me. That was the first time I cried in front of him and he didn't freeze up or power down like a laptop. We were still in each other's lives off and on for three more years.

It took me way too long to cut this man from my life, but eventually, in February 2016, I did it. I was moving to Los Angeles, pursuing acting, and I was done. One of the last things I said to him before I moved was, "You took my twenties; you cannot have my thirties."

I still have not figured this shit out, but I am trying.

Between The Mechanic and UPS guy, around fall of 2009, there was Baby Suge. The very sweet felon who loved me. He was the best boyfriend I ever had. He wanted to give me everything, but since he was a felon he couldn't give me much. He couldn't even get his own apartment because the State of Georgia did not allow convicted felons to get an apartment in their name. I broke up with him because he started doing illegal shit. He was a goon with a heart of gold. And then there was James. He was the longest labeled relationship I ever had. Unfortunately he cheated on me on a night The Mechanic was fixing my car, because he said he felt inadequate that he couldn't do it even though he was in no way trained to fix a car. After I broke up with him, he started stalking me. Fun. So here I am, nine years later. Single as fuck. The last boyfriend I had resented my success and stalked me. I was lamenting to my best friend about this and he said, "You might not have been in a 'relationship,' but you haven't been single." Touché, Ben. Touché.

And we all know the apps are trash. I went on six first dates after Covid lockdown ended and I was happy to not go on a second. I think I've gotten to a point where I realize that not all attention is good attention. Now I have guys on Bumble telling me they bet they're funnier than my friends. What? My friends have HBO stand-up specials. They tour. I don't think so, sir. I don't know what I'm doing, but I know what I did, and I don't want to repeat those things, like dealing with someone because I don't want to be by myself.

I no longer have the time to just have somebody hanging around. In my twenties it was fine, but now I'm traveling and on the road. I spent a month in London. You have to be of means to come to London and come see me! I'm tired of having someone fill space. I don't know who this future man is or whether he's coming or not. I just want an equal, someone who can come to London to see me. I'm not asking anybody to fly to Bali. Can you afford Montréal? Cancún? Los Angeles?

On the CNN New Year's special when I said *No more broke dick* to Don Lemon, I meant no more penis from a man who has no money. JetBlue can get you to Puerto Rico for about two hundred dollars. I'm not asking a man to fly me first class to Korea. You can keep me in this hemisphere, baby boy. The Bahamas is the most accessible place from New York. It's not that hard.

People think being alone or lonely is hard, but hoping you're not going to be lonely is harder. Waiting and praying for somebody that you don't know is coming is hard. Hope is harder than anything. So, in the summer of 2022, I got my eggs frozen. It was all Eva Longoria's fault.

I booked my first lead role in a TV pilot, and I was playing Eva's best friend. Before I got the role, I had to do an audition and callback, and then what they call a chemistry test, where they film you and your costar so they can make sure you vibe on camera. The sound person is supposed to attach the little microphone to an actor's clothing, but this was right when Me Too was about to explode, and every male in Hollywood feared for their lives. The sound guy walks up to Eva, looking terrified.

"You can attach it to the back of my bra," Eva says.

The sound guy puts his hands up like he's in a stickup in an old Western.

"Oh no. I'm not comfortable with that," he said.

"It's fine!"

"I can't."

So at this point I look up at this paranoid little man, take the mic, and attach it to Eva's bra.

I applaud him for being respectful, but he was holding her up! I told him I'd clip my own mic to my pants, because I didn't want him to hold me up, too.

We started the chemistry read, and I noticed that Eva was blinking, hard. Was she sending me a signal? Then I saw that she had a piece of hair tangled and wrapped around her eyelashes.

"Hold on! Don't move," I said. "Do you mind if I pull this hair away for you?"

"No, thank you so much," she said. So I untangled Eva Longoria's hair and nailed the chemistry test.

Later on, when we were on set actually shooting the pilot, we were waiting around for the next take.

"How old are you?" Eva asked.

"I'm thirty-three."

"Do you want to have kids?"

"Yes, I do."

"Freeze your eggs while you're young."

"That sounds expensive."

"Don't do it today, but get the money, and get it done. You won't regret it."

I thank her for teaching me about it. But it's been a hard road, Miss Eva!

Like getting a NuvaRing or an IUD (which two gynos refused to prescribe because of my age and race), I had to convince doctors to let me freeze my eggs. They kept telling me my BMI was too high, and they didn't want to give me anesthesia. Excuse me, I watch *My 600-Lb. Life*, I know they are not getting a gastric bypass without anesthesia. Finally, after being depressed and going through two mental breakdowns, I found a doctor who said yes.

I talk to The Mechanic very rarely, because he is married with a child. Recently I did have a moment of healing from him. He finally saw me do stand-up. We were two years in when I started doing comedy, and he never came to see me. Even when I was hosting one of his favorite comedians, Donnell Rawlings, he still wouldn't come. Yes, yes, I should have walked away. But when you convince yourself you can't do better than your current situation, you put up with a lot of nonsense. I was confident in my career, but never confident with men. If you were a fat girl during the time I grew up, you were friends with boys, and that's it. Or if they liked you, it was a secret. So with The Mechanic, that childhood insecurity stuck.

On January 20, 2023, I opened for Trevor Noah at the Fox Theatre in Atlanta, and The Mechanic was in the audience with his wife. He texted me to congratulate me, and I couldn't believe it. I met up with him and his wife after the show.

"What are you doing here?" I asked.

"Well, I figured you would be here, since you and Trevor are so tight at the desk."

The look on his wife's face was amazing. There was definitely going to be a conversation about his comment on the way home. He said he bought his tickets two or three months before the show, but I didn't know I was even going to be on the show until two DAYS before. LOOK AT GOD! Bringing us back together. I told him that the Fox Theatre was a better way to see me than the dive bars I was performing at when I first started.

"Did you perform at the SweetWater 420 Fest when Snoop Dogg was there?" asked his wife.

I said I did but then quickly changed the subject. I could not fathom the idea of his wife seeing me do stand-up almost ten years before he did. Atlanta is the smallest big city in America. We didn't talk for long because I was running late to have dinner with friends, but in the car I almost cried. I didn't realize how cathartic that experience was for me. A past hurt that I thought I had dealt with years ago was finally healed. All those times he told me he was going to come see a show, and we both knew he was lying, and he finally came. This time, was he in a relationship? Yes, but he came. I didn't know that I needed that, but I'm glad I got it.

So here I am. I'm in therapy, eggs frozen, career booming, pledging No More Broke Dick on live TV to anyone who can hear. I am tired of fantasizing about this dream man. Where is he? I don't know who he is or what he looks like, but he's late.

WHAT DID HE SAY?

I love men, but they have said some of the dumbest shit to me over the years, so in this list I'll explain it all, or try to. . . .

- *"What's an aquarium?"* I went to the Georgia aquarium for my twenty-fifth birthday with my mom, and when I told my then boyfriend, Baby Suge, he actually asked, "What's an aquarium? Is it like a museum?" I said yes . . . for fish. I had sex with this man.

- *"I'm trying to get the sperm out."* But I told you all about this earlier.

- *The LeVar Burton/Lance Button mix-up.* The Mechanic, again. He did not know that the Black dude from *Reading Rainbow* was NOT a white magician. I had to explain this.

- *"I could tell you had an ass from the front."* This pickup line needs no explanation.

- *"I don't really fuck with the internet?"* This question was asked in this century, not in 1912.

- *"You really be fucking with them white boys."* Charming.

- *"You're a big girl, you should be glad men are even talking to you."* See the shit I deal with?

- *"What makes you think you deserve a high-quality man?"* PASS.

- *"You're a THESPIAN? I thought you liked dudes."*

- *"You're pretty, for a Black girl."* This one is always fun!

FIVE

I'm a Woman in Comedy and I Do Just Fine

Everything changed for me in 2015. Maybe not everything. I didn't grow seven inches taller, marry a prince, or take up the banjo, but I did make strides as a woman in the boys' club known as stand-up comedy. Yes, I was still working during the day, but I was also getting onstage at night and beating a bunch of men in competitions and festivals. People (mostly white women) say it's tough to get respect as a woman in comedy, but not for me. I get respect all day long—except for those Atlanta show bookers who wouldn't put me on because they had "already had one female on the show and we don't need more than that." I'm sure y'all think I remember *all your names*, but I don't. Why would I? It is interesting that some of those bookers will message to say they are proud of me or some other lie whenever I get another advancement in my career. Beat it, loser.

Most men won't sleep with you if they respect you, and I got respect from a lot of male comics! Meaning, even if I *wanted* to have sex with one of them, they'd say, "Oh, yeah . . . I see you as a peer. I *respect* you." And comics in the greenroom don't assume I'm the girlfriend of a comedian, which I always thought was interesting. If they see me in there, they assume I am there to work, because if they don't want to date me, why would any other man on the show? So if I'm in the greenroom I'm either a comic or an industry executive (the logic is wild, but anyway). This pisses off some female comics who are always complaining about sexism and being harassed by dudes who think they can't be funny and pretty at the same time. I'm pissed because I don't know if they are including me in this pretty-girl clique. We all know I'm pretty. Have you seen my face? Bitch, I'm adorable.

It's impossible to meet a man at a comedy show. Not a

comedian, but, like, a regular guy in the audience. A group of single men don't go to comedy clubs, they go to strip clubs or bars or sporting events. Single women on the other hand LOVE comedy shows. Single women—or women who drag their significant others out—are the ones that keep comedy clubs open. So I didn't understand it when men started perpetuating the whole "women are not funny" lie, but I'm sure it was to keep us out of the clubs so they could holler at all the single women coming to shows. This is just a theory. More likely is that a man saw a woman killing it onstage and just didn't like that she was funnier than him. So he had a meeting with all the other unfunny men and they decided to keep women out of comedy. Somebody came up with that bullshit and I would love to know who and why. Like, you really think women can't be funny. Are you saying that Sam Jay isn't funny? Maria Bamford? Cristela Alonzo? Ali Wong! Fuck outta here.

2015 was a banner year for me. Let's review!

March: Laughing Skull Festival

April: Women in Comedy Festival

May: Bridgetown Festival

June: Callback for Stand Up for Diversity

July: Just For Laughs Comedy Festival—New Faces

October: NACA Central Region Tulsa

October: NACA Mid-Atlantic Buffalo

December: Finals for Stand Up for Diversity

December: I won Stand Up for Diversity

Look at that list. It changed my life! The Daniel Fast is a powerful thing.

By the way, for those of you unfamiliar with the Daniel Fast, it's a strict vegan diet based on the biblical Book of Daniel.

The first time I applied to the Laughing Skull Festival in Atlanta, I didn't get in, and the next two times I was an alternate—meaning that I didn't *really* get in. But in 2015, not only did I get into the festival, I was the only woman in the finals and I won second place.

Before that first round, when the festival had just started, I walked up to the bar to get a Sprite. I don't drink before I go onstage. Drinking makes all the jokes in my head disappear like a deadbeat dad. At the bar, there was a man standing there, making eye contact, so I said hello. He shook my hand.

"Hi. I'm Reg," he said.

"I'm Dulcé Sloan. Nice to meet you."

"Are you competing in the festival?"

"Yes, I am!" I said.

Before he had a chance to say anything else, I was whisked away by fellow comedian and competitor, Lace Larrabee.

"Girl, come on! The show is about to start!"

"Nice to meet you, Reg! Byyyye!"

I had a set to do, and I didn't know who Reg was. How was I supposed to know he was one of the judges?

My first set that night was good but not great, because I placed third. After the show I ran into Reg again, and he introduced me to one of the coordinators for Stand Up for Diversity. We remembered each other from the time I did the show back in 2012.

"Hi, good to see you again."

"Yeah, you too. I'm putting you in the callback round for Stand Up for Diversity in June."

"Oh wow, really?"

"Take out your phone. Hurry up. And email me so we can send you the info."

"So I don't have to line up again and wait outside?"

"Nope, just show up to the callback."

"That is amazing, thank you."

"Have you met these guys?"

He leads me over to three people sitting at the bar. We exchange pleasantries and then I go to find my friends. Lace stops me.

"You know you were talking to the judges, right?"

"What? No. I thought they were just industry."

"Yes, the judges are industry."

"I know that! I just didn't know it was them. So the judges were those three people?"

"Noooo! Them *plus* Reg and the guy from NBC. You were just chatting with the judges and didn't even know."

"How was I supposed to know?"

"I can't with you. I need a drink."

Third place got me into the Wild Card round. The Wild Card set was killer, and I got first place. First place in the Wild Card round advanced me to the Finals. I was waiting in a holding area next to the stage, watching the comic before me and going over my set. I was wearing leopard-print pants, a leopard-print bra, and a red peplum shirt open with a limited amount of coverage so the bra was basically the shirt. I had a wrap over the outfit so I could reveal my skintight leopard-print look when I walked onstage.

The comedian ended his set by making a joke about fat people. It wasn't groundbreaking, so I was like, whatever, I am focusing on my set. I have heard this shit before. But then he just keeps going and he is not doing well. I stopped going over my set, looked toward the stage, and focused in on what this man was saying. I could see people's faces out in the audience, and there were lots of plus-size people in that room, and I am a plus-size person, so I knew their looks well. My goal went from just winning the competition to winning and making sure that man didn't even place.

He came into *my* city and is talking shit? Fuck that! I could feel about ten Atlanta comics looking at me like, "Bitch, he's in your city talking shit. WHAT ARE YOU GONNA DO?"

Sometimes a comedian who goes up before you will talk about something that inspires you to go up and riff on what they said. Sometimes it's fun and good-natured, but this was not that. I hung on this dude's every dumb, offensive word, looking for my "in." He started talking about tired fat-people catchphrases like "more cushion for the pushin'," which no one has said since the 1990s, by the way. I knew just what to do. I was gonna get his ass.

He did his closing joke and walked offstage, but he'd sucked all the energy out of the room and killed the crowd. The poor MC went out there and tried his best to bring the crowd back, but that's not easy to do in sixty seconds.

After trying and failing to get the crowd ready for me, he shouted, "Ladies and gentlemen . . . welcome Dulcé Sloan!"

Before I walk onstage, I notice a table of Black uncles next to me. I throw my wrap off and see that *that* got their attention, which is a start. I'm onstage in my leopard-print bra and my tight leopard leggings, I grab the mic, and I say:

"I got your cushion, motherfucker."

The whole crowd (including all the judges) jumped out of their seats and into an applause break. I put my hand up like a choir director, and I got them all shushed, since now I only had six minutes for my set. If a set is timed but they don't have a little light off to the side to notify you when your time is almost up, I'll set the timer on my phone and stick it in my bra, on vibrate, so I know when I have thirty seconds left. The crowd was so energetic and wild during my set that night, I didn't even feel the alarm. When I walked offstage, I went straight to the bathroom because I was shaking so much. There were about six comics on after me, and I don't even remember if I watched their sets. I do know that I did not care if I placed. Bringing that dude down was my main motivation. Being a woman in comedy is not that hard—as long as you know how to take a dude down.

At the after-party that night, Reg came up and told me he

wanted to meet with me—at eight a.m. for coffee. It was currently almost three a.m., but I made sure I woke up and went. If I'd known he was a manager when I met him earlier, maybe I would have bought him a Sprite. We set a place for the next morning, and a dude I was hanging out with prepared me for the meeting, asking me questions he figured a manager would ask. It was sweet of him, but then he kept coming back to me over the next year asking me if I could help get Reg to be his manager, too. I mentioned it, but my manager was not interested, and that dude wouldn't let it go. I don't hang out with him anymore, but I am glad he prepared me because otherwise I would have gone in there looking like a fool.

Reg asked me why I liked stand-up (I love performing) and what goals did I have for my career (to be a full-time actor and comedian). I'm just a nice Southern girl, I didn't know that Reg or the company he worked for were a big deal, but I must have done all right, because he offered to manage me, and after we met we got on a conference call with his boss, Miss Jane, who I love to this day. I signed with Reg right then and there.

Another opportunity I got from the Laughing Skull Festival was that I was chosen for the New Faces of Comedy at the Just For Laughs Comedy Festival in Montréal, Canada. The standard way that comics get New Faces is that they do a set at an audition showcase and then do a different set at a callback showcase, and then wait to find out if they have been chosen. I wasn't selected that way. I did a set during the first round, did another set for the Wild Card round, and did the best jokes from both rounds at the Finals. In June, Reg called me and said I was going to Canada. I don't talk about it often because comics think I am bragging or being an asshole. But I'm not; I'm just telling what happened. And I hadn't heard of New Faces until a year before when a comedian from Atlanta got it. They didn't have auditions in Atlanta until 2015, and they were happening at the same time as the Laughing Skull Festival. I actually switched shows with another comedian who was auditioning for New Faces, and his Laughing Skull set conflicted. He said I was the only comic that was willing to switch with him. Which I thought was crazy because it didn't matter which show you were on, you were still competing.

I didn't have time to buy new clothes for my sets at JFL, so Reg took me shopping.

"Do you want me to hang back, or do you want the boyfriend experience?" he asked.

It had been so long since I had a boyfriend that I almost forgot what it was like. "The boyfriend experience, of course."

There were no plus-size stores in sight, so I guess there are no full-bodied bitches in Montréal. We ended up at Old Navy and I got three shirts. A sheer coral-and-white long-sleeved shirt that I wore for a comedy vlog interview, a black-and-white light-knit tank, and a long-sleeved black shrug that I still wear all the time. Reg's assistant would always say that I was his favorite. What can I say? Sorry? But that would be a lie. *Hehehe*.

The year of our Lord 2015 kept on going this way, and I started needing more time off from my stucco job, which led to my boss telling me it was time to go. She did let me take off thirteen days to do all those festivals, instead of the five days I had for the year. She meant this in the most encouraging way, and she was right, and I owe her that car for all her support. While I was doing all these shows at night and selling stucco during the day, I would sneak into my car or a friend's car in the parking lot to take a nap. I would change clothes and do my makeup in the bathroom or sometimes in my car, depending on the venue. It was not glamorous, and it was not easy.

I left the stucco behind and headed to NBC's Stand Up for Diversity competition (now called StandUp NBC) in December. It's a yearly competition where NBC chooses a few cities to hold auditions to find the next big thing when it comes to diverse comics. In 2012, I stood in a long-ass line to try out for Stand Up for Diversity like all the other Atlanta comedians, and I didn't get past the callback round. Now I was starting the process *at* the callback round? That Daniel Fast be working, Jack! You know who has won Stand Up for Diversity in the past? W. Kamau Bell, Michelle Buteau, and Tone Bell, among many others. And I love Michelle Buteau. She is trying to help me on my journey to find a husband AND she gave me the courage to believe I could write this book. God bless her and her whole family.

NBC flew me and the other finalist out to sunny Los Angeles and put us up in a nice hotel. And the finale—or as they called it, the industry showcase—was December 1. They called it an industry showcase because the room was full of agents, managers, studio execs . . . You know, the usual people that can change your life. My set went great. So great that a casting director in the audience called me in for an audition the next day. All my comedian friends told me that no one in the history of this competition has found out they won before the holidays. Here I am expecting to have the "awkward Christmas" all my friends keep telling me I'm about to have. Like, I'll spend the entire holiday and New Year's Eve checking my phone every six minutes for news. The day after the competition ended, my manager got a call. Then he called me.

"Are you sitting down?"

"Should I be? I mean I'm having lunch. What's up?"

"You won."

"Whatchu' mean I won? They said they don't announce the winner until January!"

"Well, they said they knew clearly who the winner was and didn't need to wait."

"So I just won twenty thousand dollars and a deal with NBC?"

"Yes, you did!"

"I GOTTA CALL MY MOM!"

They weren't going to announce the winner until later, so we had to keep it quiet. I told my mom, of course, but I didn't make any big announcements and I held that secret in while I did a few shows in the South. Throughout my entire career, if something good happens, my car will fuck up. It's a telltale sign. So about a week after that call from Reg, I'm driving back to Atlanta from a show in Tennessee, and I get a flat tire. My gut was telling me to pull off the road. I saw a Walmart off the highway and thought maybe I should go, but then I thought, *Nah, you don't need nothing, just go home.* I pass the exit, get a fourth of a mile down, and realize I'm driving on a flat tire. I pull over and immediately have to pee. I'm trying to figure out how and where I can pee, and how am I going to change this flat with people flying past me at seventy-five miles per hour (the flat was on the driver's side). My phone starts to blow the fuck up with texts and calls. NBC had just put out the press release saying I'd won, and I had friends and random comedians coming out of the woodwork to text me.

A friend of mine called and screamed, "YOU WON! How do you feel?!"

"Like I'm on my period and I need to pee but I'm stranded on the highway in north Georgia. Other than that, I'm fine."

"Oh."

Eventually I peed on the passenger side of my car. I used a towel from my trunk to hide myself from all the cars going southbound and the car door to shield me from the eyes of all the cars going northbound, and I had baby wipes in my purse. Since becoming a comedian I have peed outdoors more times than I ever thought I was going to, so I always have the wipes.

I was in the middle of changing the tire when an older

white man in a pickup that's towing a lawn mower pulls over behind my car.

"Hi," he says, like we have an appointment and it's no big deal that he's here.

"Hello, sir. Thank you so much! I've been . . ."

"Stand on the other side of the car."

He did not want to have a conversation, which was fine by me because I didn't want to distract him and make him forget a lug nut. So he silently changed my tire, and off he went.

"Thank you, sir!" I called after him.

"Yep."

If a woman needs help, a Southern gentleman will pull off the side of the road and help her. That man might have been an old racist at heart or maybe he marched with Dr. King, I don't know. I don't want to assume. I don't know that man. But thank the Lord he was so programmed by Southern chivalry that he couldn't help himself. An angel in khaki shorts and white New Balances. Like a robot programmed to assist a lady, he fixed my tire so I could get back to the 560 texts I'd gotten.

When you win Stand Up for Diversity, it's kind of like the whole next year you're a pageant winner, and you must perform duties during your reign. You host showcases and events, go to parties, and attend fancy dinners. At one of these dinners toward the end of my reign, I was at a table of about twenty comedians. I had an awful cold, so my plan was to eat some sushi, go to my hotel room, and go to bed. This was before Covid, back when people with awful colds would still go to fancy restaurants and not get murdered by the glares of others. There was a female comic at the opposite end of the table from me, talking loudly about how hard it was to get respect as a woman in comedy, how everybody wants to have sex with you, and they all doubt you have talent. I'm just eating my sushi, minding my business, trying not to sneeze, when she brings my name into the conversation.

"Isn't that right, Dulcé?"

All nineteen heads at the table whipped around to look at me.

"What?" I mumbled as I ate my tuna roll.

"If you are in the greenroom, they just assume you are someone's girlfriend."

"No one assumes I'm someone's girlfriend."

I could tell this girl was not happy with me. To this day we don't speak. But don't put your narrative on my narrative. I worked my ass off to get to that table—I served fried shrimp and hush puppies at Long John Silver's for fuck's sake—but no one ever assumed I was the girlfriend when I was at comedy shows, and I wasn't going to lie or let anyone hijack my story. This girl thought I was trying to be shady when she was looking for solidarity, but I was just being honest. I also just wanted some Sudafed and a pillow. I did shut the whole table down, which was fine with me because that meant that maybe I could go to bed sooner.

It's not like I *never* experienced sexism as a woman in comedy. Remember those bookers who just couldn't put more than one female at a time up on a show? Not to mention male comics calling me "intimidating" before I have even said a word. If you are in a male-dominated industry and most of those men don't want to sleep with you, then there is a level of bullshit that you don't have to deal with. But do they still doubt your ability because you are a woman? Yes. Do they openly debate whether women are funny if you or any other woman on a show has a great set? Of course. And do they resent you when you get good opportunities and advance in your career? Absolutely. Because how dare I be good at what I do?!? Well, I dare, sirs. I dare.

SIX

Don't Jump Out of a Moving Car

It is not wise to jump out of a moving car that's going sixty miles per hour. Not that I've tried, but I have damn sure wanted to. Being an up-and-coming comic means you're constantly on the road. Being a successful comic also means you're constantly on the road, except the snacks and the transportation get better. Instead of Chili Cheese Fritos and a Chevy Cavalier with no A/C, you're eating peanuts on an airplane. Eventually you do make it to first class, and you try to forget getting pulled over by the cops as cans of energy drinks roll around in the backseat.

Remember energy drinks? People used to get wild on energy drinks. And there used to be more than just caffeine in them. They put something called "wormwood" in some of them, until that ingredient got banned in a bunch of states for making people black out and do dumb shit all over the country. The night I got pulled over in a car with a bunch of fools drinking energy drinks, they were still full of wormwood, which is one of the reasons I wanted to jump out of a speeding car on a dark highway in Georgia.

It was 2012, and I had one of my first headlining shows. It was at a bar in Augusta, Georgia, and I was doing thirty minutes, which, to be only three years in, meant it was not going to be the strongest thirty-minute set in the history of comedy, since I had very little experience. I got a ride to the show from some baby comics who were also performing, and they picked me up in a late 1990s Jeep Wrangler that had seen much better days. Why I let these two stoned white boys drive me two hours across the state is beyond me, but I had a show to get to. When they pulled up, I opened the door and a cloud of weed smoke billowed out as though Martha Stewart and Snoop Dogg were inside. A bunch of pill bottles rattled around on the floorboard, so instead of giving them a polite hello I peered inside the car and said:

"Excuse me, but what are y'all doing in here?"

"Huh?"

Maybe they were too stoned to realize they were drunk, so I told them to get their asses in the back so the grown-up (me) could drive. I wanted to be sitting in the back in peace, going over my set, and not talking about who could fart the loudest, Thing or the Hulk, but instead I had to drive two hours and babysit Dumb and Dumber. Anyway, as I drove and they tumbled around in the back, I looked at the gas gauge and saw that we were almost on empty.

"Hey."

They didn't hear me because they were too busy singing Justin Bieber songs.

I turned the radio down, but they kept on singing.

"HEY!"

"Huh?"

"We're almost out of gas."

"Oh, no, the gas gauge is messed up. You're fine."

Okay, cool. I asked because I saw a gas station at the next exit and was going to stop and get gas. But I believed these fools, and I kept going. I should have listened to my instincts, my gut, my first mind—whatever you want to call it—because as soon as I drove past the off-ramp and under the overpass, the car started sputtering and ran out of gas. I pulled over on the side of the freeway. One of the idiots in the back asked, "Whoa, what happened?"

"We ran out of gas," I said, trying to keep my composure.

"Oh, that's weird. I drive around all the time on E and usually it's fine."

"Well, not today. Do you have a gas can in the back?"

"Huh?"

I took that as a no.

I had to pee, but I was not going to do it in front of these fools, so I walked up the on-ramp, to the gas station I should have stopped at, peed, bought a gas can, and bought gas, in that order. I walked back with that can, cursing my passengers, and berating myself in my head. Why did they think it was okay to pick me up high and drunk and then drive two hours through country-ass Georgia? Why didn't I trust my instincts and go to the gas station? I got back to the car and I popped open the tank to fill it up so we wouldn't miss the show. Did I mention that they were both under twenty-one? There was a door-like flap on the gas tank that wouldn't open with the nozzle on the gas can. So I found a pen in the car and used it to push the flap back, but I couldn't fit the pen and the nozzle through the flap at the same time. I needed a funnel. As if I needed any more trouble, a Georgia Highway Patrol car rolls up and parks behind us. The officer gets out.

"Is everything all right?" the cop asked.

I looked inside the car full of energy drinks, smoke, and pills and thought, yeah, everything is fine, besides the two-man *Wolf of Wall Street* reenactment happening in the backseat.

"Everything's fine, officer!"

I still needed a funnel to get this gas in the car so we could get to the gas station to get more gas so we could make it to the show. The idiots didn't have a funnel and neither did the cop, so I had to improvise. There were empty bottles and trash all over the car, so I cut a sixteen-ounce soda bottle in half with the box cutter I keep in my purse (much to the shock of the cop) and I used it to funnel gas into the car.

I thanked the cop for his headlights and flash and I told him we were just fine and thank you so much and please get back into your damn cruiser before you start asking for IDs and throw us all in jail. By some miracle the cop let us go on our way. Maybe he sympathized because I told him I was headlining a comedy show and people needed me. Maybe he was about to end his shift and didn't want to deal with arresting anyone just as he was about to clock out. Whatever the reason, I got back in that car and drove like hell to Augusta so we could do the show and then go home. The booker had been blowing up my phone trying to get an ETA on when we would be there. We are late! We are gonna be late, sir! I had to MacGyver gas into a car!

We got there, and Dumb and Dumber did their sets first. I got called up and started telling the story of our journey to the show that night. Sometimes you have a plan, and God hands you two fools and an empty tank of gas and you need to seize the moment. Not long after I got onstage, some older Black man, a true Uncle, started heckling me. I tried to ignore him at first, hoping he'd just get tired of being ignored and shut his ass up, but he kept at it. At one point he yelled, "Oh yeah, girl! We got two hard dicks right here and we'll take you in the bathroom right now!"

At some bars, a bouncer or manager might pounce on this heckler and shut him down or kick him out, but not at this fine establishment. Apparently he was a regular, so folks told him to quiet down, but no one asked him to leave. He kept on going, so I flipped out on this dude. I'd just endured a two-and-a-half-hour nightmare, so I was not about to stand there while this walking disappointment ruined my set *and* disrespected me. I always carry a knife/box cutter in my purse, just like my mom always carries a gun. I'm not going back and forth with you once you threaten me.

"Sir, there is a knife in my purse and I will use it."

"Oh, what?" He laughed. "You gonna cut off my dick?"

"No, sir. I'm gonna give you a new smile from ear to ear."

As soon as I said it, this man starts crying. Like, bawling like a newborn baby. I finished my set and walked offstage, ready to get the hell home to Atlanta.

After my set, the heckler's friend comes up to me and starts telling me how upset this guy is, how much I scared him. He was actually trying to get me to apologize!

"That man threatened to assault me. Fuck him," I said. "What the hell do I have to apologize for?"

Then the heckler wanders over and tells me he's sorry. I told him to step aside. Why should I accept an apology from a man who fifteen minutes before was suggesting sexual assault like it was a good time? I found Dumb and Dumber talking to some girls, and they refused to leave the bar. I had the keys to their car, and I had to get back that night because I had to be at my day job in the morning. I told them I was driving back to Atlanta whether they got in the car or not. They said goodbye to the girls, stumbled outside, passed out in the back, and I drove back to my house. I think I made maybe one hundred dollars that night.

I've driven through rainstorms, over potholes, and across state lines for a show. I've stayed in motels and hotels in Mobile, Alabama, and Arlington, Texas. I don't daydream about leaping out of every car I'm in, but being a comedian means being on the road, and sometimes those roads are paved with memories of alcohol and nonsense. One of the 8,000 steps to becoming what some people see as an "overnight success" in comedy involves doing the college circuit, and it's an experience that a lot of comics never speak about. Maybe because it's so fucking ridiculous.

When I signed with my manager in 2015 after I got second place at the Laughing Skull Festival, I also got a college agent, who helps you book shows at campuses around the country so you can get more exposure and hopefully better gigs where grown men don't threaten to drag you into a bathroom. From November 2015 to April 2017 I probably performed at sixty schools. My longest run was hitting thirteen schools in fourteen days, in six states, stretching from Maine to Delaware. My best friend, Ben, or I would drive all over the East Coast trying to make drunk nineteen-year-old students laugh. I almost died multiple times driving in ice and snow, almost flipping onto embankments, hydroplaning, and skidding across rickety old bridges. This is what overnight success looks like.

On the college circuit you have to do these showcases sponsored by NACA, which stands for National Association for Campus Activities. The students watch your set and bid on the comic they want, through the comic's agent. It's tiring as hell but a good way to hone your set and learn what works and what bombs. Once I was backstage at one of these showcases, and there's a comic from LA that I'd never met. He's doing a joke and I found myself mouthing this joke word for word, like I'd memorized it. Turns out there was some kid in Atlanta who was stealing this LA comic's joke and passing it off as his own, which is why I knew it word for word. I told the LA comic about the Atlanta guy stealing his joke, just so he'd know there was a thief out there.

When I went back to Atlanta, I didn't want to be the one causing drama, so I told the one comic who I knew was the town crier, and I let him spread the news. The thief was some rich kid. He started working at one of the comedy clubs in the city and booked himself as the host all the time but didn't have the ten to fifteen minutes of material he needed since he just started, so he went online and stole jokes from other Indian or Middle Eastern comics.

What made me and other comics so mad was that not only did he steal from other comics of color, but he was taking money out of the hands of comics that could have been doing the hosting spots he kept putting himself in. There was eventually a whole blowup when everyone found out he was a thief, and he called me crying. Like I was going to help. He explained what happened and why he did it and blah, blah, blah. Young man, please get off the phone I pay the bill on. And he didn't need to apologize to me! He needed to apologize to the comics he stole from. I'm just trying to protect my community.

He disappeared after that. I don't mean he disappeared like some comic blindfolded him, drove him to an empty field at night, and sent him to Jesus. I mean he gave up comedy and probably went to work for his dad. Maybe my detective skills caused that kid to rethink his priorities and I saved him from a lifetime of bombing onstage. We'll never know, unless he reads this book and sends me a DM.

The college circuit was exhausting, since you have to talk to the students and answer a million questions in between traveling and trying to locate a single building on a campus of eight hundred buildings. The hardest part of those college tours was the fact that they always gave one address for the entire campus, like 2300 University Drive, but then you're confused, running around trying to find the Performing Arts Center, Student Union Building, or Cafetorium, which might be a mile away from that generic address. Then you perform, you talk to the students, and if you don't talk to them because you're tired and all you've eaten that day is an old granola bar you took from the motel lobby, they give you a bad score. The positive side, besides the exposure, is that you do get paid, and it's not a hundred bucks. I have a friend who paid off their student loans with the money they made doing colleges, so it's worth it to spend some time acting like a hooker on a stroll through the hallowed institutions of higher learning.

I met my friend Josh Johnson doing the NACA thing, and we wound up on *The Daily Show* together, and now we have a podcast called *Hold Up* (which you've listened to, right?).

The week before I did my first college show was the scariest because I had to quit my job. My steady-paycheck day job at the stucco company. Now, remember, Abbey let me take thirteen days off at work to go to comedy festivals and NACA showcases. She believed in me and would defend me to the big boss about giving me all that time off. But the day finally came when I used up all my days and chances. If I was going to do this show, I was going to have to take a leap of faith.

"Abriella! I booked my first college show!"

"Congratulations! When is it?"

"Tuesday."

"You can't take any more days off for the rest of the year."

"Really?"

"Yes. I let you take eight more days than you were supposed to."

"What am I going to do?"

"You have to give your two-week notice."

"Wait, what?"

"You have to quit. Give me your notice."

"But it's not even two weeks. And what am I going to do for work when I get back?"

"You are going to have more shows. Don't worry."

I *was* worried. I had money in the bank, so I was fine, but I was finally in the place I had wanted to be in my whole life and I still didn't know what to do.

J. P. was a talent booker, a silver fox of a man. I'd met him at the Bridgetown Comedy Festival and then Just For Laughs, and he saw me onstage at NBC's Stand Up for Diversity. I got a call one day a few months after we'd met, out of the blue.

"Hey, Dulcé, this is J. P., I'm not sure if you remember me. . . ."

"Oh, sure . . ."

I had no clue who was on my phone.

"There's a comedy showcase for Turner I think you'd be great for. . . ."

"Sounds great."

Hell yes! I had just quit my day job and I'd been praying to Jesus to give me a sign that this whole comedy thing was going to be worth quitting stucco sales for.

J. P. invited me out to LA for a showcase, and they flew me out and put me up in a hotel. I did this Turner comedy showcase about a week after Stand Up for Diversity. J. P. told me to come by *Conan* the next day, so I was like, cool, all the comedians doing this showcase are probably invited to watch a taping. That's nice. So I show up for this "taping," and I'm sitting in this office with J. P. when the door opens and Conan walks in. The man is like seventy-five feet tall, as tall as Tyler Perry, who is also seventy-five feet tall. I keep it cool and we're talking, and then J. P. goes over to a whiteboard with a calendar on it and picks up a marker.

"I think we can get you on in March," he says.

Now I'm freaking out. I want to scream, "Abso-fucking-lutely, you gorgeous man," but instead I say something like, "Sure, that sounds feasible."

After the Important Meeting, which was not a taping after all, I called my manager, Reg, yelling into the phone that I JUST BOOKED *CONAN*.

"Why did you think you were there?" he said.

"To watch a taping!"

"Dulcé . . . "

So yeah, I was doing *Conan*.

Then Reg called me at the end of January.

"I know J. P. said March, but they want you sooner."

"What's sooner?" I asked. Hoping he would say February 28.

"In two weeks."

When we hung up I called my mom into my room.

"Mommy? I'm going on *Conan* in two weeks."

"I told you good things come to you when you do the Daniel Fast," she said. Abbey introduced me to this fast when we did it together in January of 2015. As of January 2016 I was a full-time comedian. So I had evidence that opportunities come when I do this fast. It's a religious fast where you eat strictly vegan foods for twenty-one days. And not just vegan. No sugar, no alcohol, no bread, nothing with yeast. You can only drink water, and if you aren't married, no sexy time. I don't know if no sexy time is a real stipulation, because it is not in the Bible with all the restrictions listed in Daniel 10:3. Abbey made a valid point about that. Technically, I shouldn't be unmarried and fornicating anyway. And to that I said, "Technically yes, but God knows my heart."

Anyway, Abbey was right. Good things happened when I did the Daniel Fast, because now I was about to get on TV in front of millions of people, and instead of being judged by a bunch of college kids, I was being judged by America and Conan O'Brien. Harvard grad, beloved comedian, and late-night giant. Really. The man is tall as fuck.

When you're doing late night, you can't just walk onstage and say whatever you want, surprising the producers and the American public with a story about your favorite orgy or your stolen sex tape—or no more broke dick.

Instead, you have to submit transcripts of your set, tape your set, and let them see it on camera, word for word. You write every syllable down so they can make sure no one is saying something that will get the network fined by the FCC. So I recorded my whole set. I did talk about my bra, about gay men grabbing my boobs at brunch, a grocery store employee insulting me, and white women touching my Afro (yes, THIS HAPPENS). I had to do the TV-friendly version of those jokes, not the club version, but it still hit. Changing the word "fuck" to "sex" didn't kill the joke. The essence was still there. Plus I got to shut down all the white people who'd tell me, "White women don't touch your Afro, that doesn't happen." YES IT FUCKING DOES!

Picking your outfit for your first big TV appearance is serious business. I went straight to Rainbow clothing store with my mom, who told me to wear high-waisted pants to hide my stomach and emphasize my chest because my shirt was black lace paired with a leopard bra. My hair and makeup were on point (thank you to Conan's glam team), and to prepare, I told myself that this was not a big deal. It was just another gig, like all the other gigs I'd done for years in Asheville, Atlanta, Mobile, Chattanooga, and Augusta. Yeah, Conan would be watching, and there wouldn't be any hecklers in the audience because TV tapings have tight security. It was just a show. Only way, way more intense. But if I told myself anything other than "This is not a big deal" I would have gotten too into my head, and maybe fucked it all up. So I lied to myself!

I was a theater kid, so I had no problem sticking to a script or finding my light—I played the Diva in *Starmites*, remember? I could handle pretty much anything. As hard as I tried to be calm, though, I was nervous as hell standing in the wings, waiting to go on. I will never forget a stagehand handing me a microphone and holding the curtain for me who said, "You got this. You've done this a thousand times." And calm came rushing over me!

Sir, I will give you a baby if you ask. Just say the word. Then I went out there and killed it.

Once I walked offstage, and after Conan very nicely told me to let him know if I needed anything or if I ever wanted to come on the show again, I finally let it all hit me: I JUST DID *CONAN*. That show was kind of a springboard for my whole career, so no, it did not happen "overnight." I didn't move to Los Angeles and book *Conan* the next day. No one watching, except my mom and my friends, knew about the energy-drink car rides or the bar shows or the college tours where I drove over ice and snow just to get to a gig.

I still hustle to this day. Maybe the cars are better, and I'm in first class, but I still tour ALL THE DAMN TIME. As a comedian you always have to be ready to go onstage, even if you're not booked for a show. You might be watching some friends onstage and then someone says, "Hey, why don't you hop on for five minutes. . . ." You have to be prepared at all times, like a Jedi. I am tired as hell, but if you ask me to go up onstage, 80 percent of the time I'm going to say I'll do it. I'll drive to gigs, fly to clubs, walk onstage, and deliver. That's what I signed up for, and this "overnight success" has been working her damn ass off, every day, for years. The way folks talk about my career, you would think it was a daylight robbery.

SEVEN

No, I'm Not a Writer
on *The Daily Show*

Some people might say it's a bad idea to stick to your religious fast on your first day of work at a major TV show/cultural phenomenon with millions of viewers like *The Daily Show*. I am not most people, though, but you probably know that by now since you are on page 165 of this book.

Before you start yelling and telling me that it's not smart to be hungry on the first day of a new job, it's not like this fast made me hallucinate or pass out. I have done this before. I didn't stare at Trevor from across the desk and imagine his arm turning into a juicy chicken wing, like a Looney Tunes cartoon character who'd just been concussed after falling off a cliff. I was allowed to have water from six in the morning to six at night, then I could have dinner. I couldn't head to Popeye's Chicken at 6:01 p.m. every day and order a Shrimp Tackle Box and a Dr Pepper, but I could have something "sensible," like grilled chicken and sautéed vegetables. So I wasn't *dying*. I was cleansing myself. But time did feel like it was going backward once five thirty p.m. came around.

Before that first day on the job, I had to audition. They didn't just call me up and hire me from my résumé. This wasn't Raybad. That's not how all this works. Comedy Central reached out to my manager and told him they wanted me to audition. I auditioned for the show back in 2015 and didn't even remember. Neither did my manager, Reg, which tells you how far I got, and it also tells you how often I was working and auditioning for other projects. I also followed the rule of thumb of "Send in the tape and forget it." You always have to remember that what is meant for you will always find you. So it makes sense that I wouldn't remember auditioning for *The Daily Show*. I don't let myself dwell on every audition I do. If I did, it would drive me mad.

This time around, in 2017, I wasn't even sure I wanted to send in an audition tape because I didn't see myself as a political comic, and *The Daily Show* IS political satire. Worse than that—if I got the job, I'd have to move to New York. I don't know why humans made New York City, or what the fucking plan was. What is New York even for? Yeah, some people love it, but some people walk on hot coals. Some people eat tomatoes. It's the same thing.

When I told my manager and agents I wasn't sure I wanted to take the job, they all started saying things like:

"What do you mean? Just try. Just try!"

"Of course you're auditioning!"

"Just see, let's just see . . . It could make you a big star."

The last comment made me mad. Don't try to gas me up and pimp me.

At the end of the day, my manager truly wouldn't let me not do the audition, so I agreed to make the tape.

I had to send in two tapes. The first was a standard self-tape, where they send a script and I have to perform it. For the second piece I had to write something that demonstrated my point of view and perform it as a "desk piece" with me and Trevor. I'm sorry, what? Y'all want me to write a piece for the show? The only things I'd ever written were some jokes, some checks, and a few grocery lists. I've never written for a TV show. I didn't want to, and frankly, I didn't know if I could. I have a degree in theater performance, not writing. But after another pep talk from Reg, I knew I couldn't quit. (Just an FYI, a talent manager's job is 30 percent giving pep talks and encouragement.) To prepare, I watched a bunch of *The Daily Show* episodes to get the format down. I had a few ideas, but I called a friend who was a writer to help me brainstorm. We came up with the idea of talking about social media. We wrote up some talking points, and I banged out a script and sent it to my manager. Reg liked it, so all I had to do was tape it. I was working in New York at the time, and a friend of mine was supposed to help me film the audition. On the day we were supposed to shoot, this friend went MIA. He ghosted me. I didn't get mad, I just figured that maybe this was a sign that it wasn't meant to be. Reg, on the other hand, did not agree. He called me the next day—the day the tape was due.

"Hey, did you get the tape done?"

"My friend who was helping was a no-show, so I couldn't."

I felt like a kid saying my dog ate my homework.

"So you aren't going to do it?"

"Well, today is the deadline, so I can't. I missed it."

"Let me call you right back."

Damn it. He called me back soon after.

"I called Comedy Central. They gave you another day."

"I don't know if I'm going to have time. I fly back to LA tomorrow and land in the afternoon, and I don't have anyone to read with me. Don't I have to have it in by end of day?"

"Don't worry about that. Just do the tape."

Reg's solution to me not having someone to read with or record with me was to read with him on Skype; he would play the role of Trevor and I would record myself on my phone. So I landed back in LA, got home as quickly as I could, and called Reg. We did the tape, I sent it to him, and now we had to wait. A few weeks later he called me and said I got a callback.

For the callback I had to write ANOTHER piece and do another pre-written script they gave me. Reg told me I needed to write about something only I could talk about. My birthday had just passed, so I decided to talk about how hard it is to be Black and have your birthday be July 4. Not only did I never have a big birthday party growing up because it is the biggest summer family holiday, but it's the day rich white men got independence from England. Independence Day wasn't for Black people or women. And I am both. I didn't have to do another tape with Reg because this time my tape was going to be with Trevor Noah. The real one, not Reg.

For the callback audition, I had to go to New York, stand in front of a green screen, and read the pre-written piece off the teleprompter. After that I would walk over to the desk and we would do the piece that I wrote. I was a *little* nervous, but I knew I had this. The only time I get nervous is if I feel unprepared, so I always prepare. Plus, I just had to be myself. Also, my nails were airbrushed red, white, and blue in a cute little Fourth of July theme since the audition was a week after my birthday. I was ready.

Trevor walked up to me, introduced himself, and said, "You're really funny." So that helped my confidence. He'd watched my stand-up! Of course he did, though. The man had to do his research. Watching my stand-up was part of his job. I did the audition, he laughed, I told everyone thank you, and then headed to the airport to fly back to Los Angeles, where I hoped to live for many, many more years.

Two hours after I left the studio, standing in front of my gate at the airport, I got a call from Reg.

"Hey, Reg."

"Hang on!"

"Okay . . . "

Then I heard a bunch of beeps, like people were joining the call in a big rush. Everyone said hello, all excited, and before I knew it there were seventeen managers, agents, and lawyers on the phone.

"Congratulations!" Reg said. "You got it!"

"I know!" I said.

"How'd you know? And I thought you'd be more excited," he said.

That's what they wanted. All those people on the phone. They wanted to hear my reaction when I got the news. And it makes sense. My manager helped me with my audition, my agents communicated with the network, and my lawyer and his staff worked on my contract, but my mind was in a different place.

"There are seventeen of y'all on the phone. Why else would everyone be here? When I don't book something it's just you, Reg." They all laughed.

"Wait! I have to move to New York?!" I exclaimed.

"Yup!"

"Ah, fuck." They all laughed again.

"Also you can't tell anybody. You have to wait for the press release when you start in September."

It was July 17. I knew how to keep my mouth shut when it came to a job or some coins. But I had to call my mom.

"Mommy, I got *The Daily Show*."

"I am so proud of you!"

"But I have to move to New York."

The last time my mom had been to New York was probably in the early 1980s. Maybe she didn't remember what I would be dealing with.

"Dulcé, it's a good job. Take the job."

I took the job, but you knew that already. And if you don't know that, you may have just found this book at a garage sale, flipped to this page, and have no idea what *The Daily Show* is because you don't own a TV. If that's you, hello, and keep reading (and get a damn TV).

One thing about being a person who has press releases written about what they're up to is that you usually have to keep your massive news a secret until the actual press release comes out. If you get a job in stucco sales or at Long John Silver's, you can scream it to your whole neighborhood through a megaphone, and no one is like, "What are you doing? You are violating your food service nondisclosure agreement!!" They're like, "Are they hiring?" So besides telling my mom and

Jesus, I kept my mouth shut about the news.

I was performing at the Just For Laughs festival two weeks after I got the job, and the place was full of comedians, agents, managers, and studio execs. I'm walking through the crowds at the Hyatt, minding my business, when I hear it.

"Congratulations, Dulcé," someone whispered.

I kept on walking since I had no idea who'd just addressed me. Then it happened again. Another whisper.

"Dulcé, congratulations."

What the hell? I know my mom didn't tell anyone at this festival, and I don't think Jesus would either. As I walked, about every ten feet someone whispered, "Heard the news, congratulations." Some strangers even shook my hand or tried to go in for a hug. I looked over at Reg, who was walking beside me.

"There are way too many white men whispering in my ear who are not trying to sleep with me."

How the hell did everybody know?

Agents and managers are the ones who tell you to wait for the press release, but they are also the ones who send mass emails through the office to hundreds of employees telling them the news. One, because people need to know who booked the jobs they are sending their clients out for, and two, because they need to be in the know and let other people know that they know. You think a bunch of agents and assistants can keep a secret? Hell no! So there I was being diligent and doing as I was told, and all these grown men were gossiping about MY business, in MY face like a bunch of men with too much time on their hands. I wind up on this big patio at the hotel, and I swear every time I looked into the crowd, someone across the room would mouth, "CONGRATS!" I wasn't allowed to tell my friends, but the entire population of the Hyatt Hotel in Montréal knew my business. The upside to this was that for the entire rest of that week, I didn't have to pay for a single meal. Not a snack, not a drink, not a pack of gum. Nothing. Why? Because multiple talent agents were trying to poach me from my current agents. I was pretty happy about all the freebies, but one of my agents, Tight Suit, was losing his shit. He was scared I was going to dump him for another agent, just because they were buying me dinner.

"Tight Suit. Chill. I am not going anywhere," I told him.

If we were at a party and I was talking to a bunch of people, he would pop up next to me like a jealous boyfriend. Even if someone handed me the keys to a Bentley with a gorgeous man inside whose only job was to do whatever the hell I asked, why would I dump the agents who believed in me from the start? I mean, I'd be tempted to take those keys. Maybe I could take the car and the man for a joy ride before I return them, but I was not going to leave Tight Suit.

I had about a month to wrap up my life in Los Angeles and move to New York. I moved to LA in February 2016. I moved into my studio apartment in September 2016 and left for New York in September 2017, for anyone who likes a fun little full-circle moment. I was subletting an apartment in Brooklyn.

I had no car and didn't know the subways, and even if I did know the subways I was not going to ride them. There are too many humans on those things. It freaks me the fuck out. I'm always worried someone is going to steal my purse or my phone or I'm going to be surrounded by men while I'm wearing a dress and end up pregnant. I would be the weirdest episode of *Maury* anyone had ever seen.

I got to work on day one, thinking my new place of business would be a fancy TV studio, but really it was an office. At the audition I'd just seen the TV studio on the first floor, so I had no clue there were actual offices. It's kind of like a newsroom situation, with cubicles and a breakroom, so it was almost just like all offices I've worked in doing customer service. I did not need more cubicles in my life. There was also zero training. When I started a new OFFICE job, which I had done A LOT, I had training. There were no big binders full of instructions, no Word documents telling you how to fix a printer jam or how to riff with Trevor. Nothing. I wasn't prepared for this. I didn't know when I was driving all over Ohio telling jokes to college students that I would once again be making small talk while smearing cream cheese on a bagel or eating the office birthday cake for all the employee birthdays that month. But I guess if it's not the service industry or live performance, a job is in an office. At least I had *my own* office, so I wasn't complaining too much. Just a little, quietly, to my mom on the phone.

"Mommy. It's an office."

"What? Really? I thought it was a TV show."

"That's downstairs. Upstairs is cubicles, breakroom, fancy coffee machines. The whole nine."

"Oooooohhh."

"Mommy! I worked hard to get out of an office, and now I have 'hard worked' myself back into an office!"

"Girl."

At the beginning, every day in this new job felt like someone had just dropped me off in the center of the running of the bulls. Dust is flying, people are screaming, and you just have to start sprinting for your life and figure the shit out so you don't get gored by a giant horn. I knew a few people on the show when I started, like Roy Wood Jr. and Michael Kosta, but other than that it was all new to me—the people (like Ronny Chieng and Desi Lydic), the place, and the rules. I had to study how the show was formatted, and then pitch bits and segments that fit into that format. It took a minute. When shit got crazy, Roy would pull me up away from the bulls, sit me on a fence, and explain how this worked or that worked. Then he'd toss me back in and tell me, "Good luck, kid," and I'd figure it out from there.

The New York comedy scene was new to me, too. I was doing stand-up in a whole new city where I could be on TV one day and performing in the basement of a pizza shop the next. I could do shows and see shows until two in the morning if I wanted to, and I loved that. Because I was on *The Daily Show*, though, a lot of white boys at these clubs wanted to sit down and talk to me and ask me how I got the gig and can I introduce them to Trevor. I didn't even know these dudes. One guy started telling me how hard it was for white dudes to make it in comedy "in this climate." I'm sorry, sir, but I am not exactly losing sleep over your so-called "oppression." At first I thought these boys were flirting, but then they'd get that look, and not a look I liked. And then it would all come out.

"It's just so hard for white guys right now. Maybe you can put in a word, or I can visit you on set and meet Trevor? You're a writer, so maybe you can help me get into the writers' room?"

"Excuse me, but—why are you telling me all this? Also—I am not a writer on *The Daily Show*."

I knew exactly why they were telling me this, but if I see a chance to taunt a fool, I take it.

"Dulcé, all I'm saying is that if the show is hiring a writer, let me know."

"Bro, please."

I didn't get *The Daily Show* because I told some comic I didn't even know to get me in the door. I had to audition, and to get that audition I had to be a good comic. One who, starting out, performed in all the states that touched Georgia and performed at colleges even after skidding across ice and snow. I put in my time. You can't just be a mediocre white man with a microphone and make it in comedy anymore. For a long time, women, people of color, and LGBTQIA+ folks have had to work twice as hard to get half as much, and now some of us are getting our due. The industry is changing and these white boys who were working half as much to get to everything are UPSET! There is so much competition in New York that people get crazy. There's also a whole legacy of the city just being HARD. Getting a gig is hard, getting noticed is hard, walking in a blizzard is hard as hell. Comedians in New York are out for blood because there is so much competition that someone really has to stand out to be noticed. It's frustrating and disheartening to see really amazing comics just struggle and question themselves and their talent, while mediocre and bad comics think that they are owed the world and are not "getting what they deserve." It is the wildest thing to watch. People say to have the confidence of a mediocre white man. No. Have the confidence of an open-mic comic who bombs all the time. They live in a castle in the sky.

If there is an industry that needs a union, it's stand-up comedy.

As a member of the Screen Actors Guild, I can say that comics face the same conditions that made actors and other performers unionize over a century ago. Consistent pay from clubs and venues, guaranteed working conditions, health insurance. What a blessing! But comics will never be able to form a union because it will be full of scabs. A scab meaning someone who refuses to join the union, or who joins and has no issue crossing a picket line. I can see it now. A group of unionized comics are protesting at a club that is underpaying comics, and another group of comics walks up saying, "If they don't want to work until everyone gets fair pay and gender equality—I'll cross the picket line and take their spot!" A lot of us are in SAG or the Writers Guild, because as your career grows you get opportunities in film and TV and need to join those unions. But if a comic just works the clubs and performs on the road, they don't have any protection, and that is a scary thought.

On another note, the greatest day in white history is when they decided to allow their dogs to come to work. If you can't see your dog because you work fourteen-hour days, then it sounds like you don't need a dog. Being back in an office was crazy enough, but having dogs there? This isn't an animal shelter. I don't work at a pet store. My coworkers just bring their dogs to work every day, like no one will care that there's a slobbering four-legged creature just wandering around licking the crumbs off the break room floor. I don't care if it's a six-pound Maltese or a ninety-five-pound pit bull, I am not a fan. I didn't want to be that new person who came to the show and then forced everyone to leave their animals at home, so I just dealt with it. Plus, I had no say. Dogs are allowed, but could I bring a fish? A pet tarantula? One woman in accounting brought her kitten to work, and that was okay because kittens are perfect little babies who need all the love and attention. And then kittens become cats. And cats don't bark at you. Also cats are better. Dogs are snitches. There, I said it. I wouldn't mind a puppy, because it's a wee baby that needs help. But full-grown dogs? Nah.

Most dogs stay in the office of their owner, but there are dogs sprawled out in hallways, blocking the stairs, dogs roaming around looking for food. There was one dog that I actually liked, so I would give him peanut butter sometimes. Then he started growling at me, maybe because my hair is always different and he couldn't handle the change. So fuck that dog. If you growl at me I ain't giving you shit. I should not have to walk into my office and be harassed by a dog!

Most of my coworkers know I am not a fan of the All Dogs Allowed policy. I don't care if they're mad about it (the dogs or the humans). Having animals growl at me is not good for my mental health. One day I'd had enough. A coworker who I'll call Kim walked into the office kitchen while I was innocently making myself a bagel. Maybe she'd just seen me give side-eye to one of the seven thousand dogs in there, because she launched right in.

"Dulcé, I don't know why you don't like dogs! Dogs are amazing and they are really sweet and . . . " She kept going on like this for another full minute that felt like an eternity.

Now usually I don't answer this question truthfully. I just give some lame excuse and keep it moving. But this was the umpteenth time that she had asked me this question, and I had time today to go off. I looked at Kim, put down my bagel like I was about to deliver the Gettysburg Address, and said, real serious, "Racist white people sicced their dog on me, Kim. When I was four years old. And again when I was ten."

"Oh . . . no . . . I'm so . . . I didn't . . ."

She backed away so fast you'd think she was on roller skates. Kim never asked me about dogs again, which is just the way I like it. After she ran away, I finished my bagel in peace.

One thing people don't realize about working on *The Daily Show* is that correspondents are always on call. Not on weekends, but on weekdays when the show is filming, I could get a call telling me to be in the office in two hours, and then I'd have to cancel auditions, recordings of *The Great North*, nail appointments, or whatever else I had planned. About 70 percent of the time, we do not know when we'll be on the show. Sometimes it's preplanned, like when we're out in the field or shooting on location in the streets. Usually, though, you have to be ready to drop everything and go hang out with all them damn dogs in the office.

Something else people might not know about the show is that anyone who works there can pitch an idea. I can pitch, a writer can pitch, a grip or camera operator can pitch. Even HR can pitch. There are over a hundred people working there, and sometimes I know exactly what someone's job is, and other times I'm like, "I've seen you hanging out here for years, but one day you're running a raffle and the next you're buying me plane tickets, so what is your job, exactly?" It takes a lot of humans to make this show, but you guys only get to see the ones on camera. If that person whose job title I don't know doesn't book the plane tickets, the correspondents can't jet out to all corners of the world to be Trevor's (and then the guest hosts') eyes and ears on the ground. Why they run raffles is not my business, but I'm sure somebody knows why they do it. Update: I asked this woman what she did so I could tell y'all and her answer was: "Whatever needs to get done for the office or you guys." Girl, what?!? How do you list that on a résumé? Because it sounds like you are a mother. A mother of the office. An office mom. If that is the case, I want orange slices and a Capri Sun. Thanks, Mom! (said like the kids in a SunnyD commercial).

If we're working on a field piece, and we go out into the world to film an interview with a gorgeous family of Black beekeepers in New Jersey or an eccentric white businessman in Wisconsin who microchips his employees, then the writers, the director, and I prepare our interview questions. They should be funny but also sound authentic to my voice. During the interview I will use the pre-written questions or ad lib in the moment if the interviewee says something that sparks a question in me. I try to work from the pre-written as much as I can, but sometimes it doesn't work. And if something doesn't work and it isn't funny and it gets on the show, it's not the writers that get blamed—it's me, or another correspondent, since we're the ones y'all see. We're the ones saying the words. If you want to know if something is funny, say it! Read it out loud. I always read things out loud, otherwise how do you know if it's any good? Read your shit out loud! If I were a writing coach, that would be my entire class: Read. Your. Shit. Out. Loud. End of lesson.

In 2018, Michael Kosta and I did a piece at Trump's Big Bad Border Walls in Mexico. We were new correspondents, and Trevor sent us packing not to Cabo or Tulum, but to lovely

Tijuana. Thank God I brought baby wipes and an airline blanket, because the director and I were the only women on the shoot, so we were peeing off to the side of a building all day with dust and trash flying everywhere. I should have been used to that shit living in New York, but in New York I could at least run into a CVS to pee. We were on the Mexico side of the wall, and when the federal police showed up to harass us, our "fixer" paid him off. Yep, we have a fixer who can step in with a wad of cash in case we're in a hostile situation and something dangerous goes down. So anyway, this was when Trump was making these proto-types for the wall, but he was being all cagey about showing the American press, so no one could get close to the prototypes on the American side. But since they were being built maybe thirty yards from the current border wall, they were easy to see from the Mexico side. Kosta and I were shooting, and at one point Kosta was standing on the roof of the fixer's SUV, yelling at the American workers trying to build these stupid things, asking them if they needed help. They didn't think we were cute or funny, and some guy flew a drone over our heads to film us. I always wondered who called the *federales* on us. A bunch of snitches.

I was interviewing a man who lived right in front of the wall and he told us he liked to get drunk, jump over the wall, give the waiting border patrol truck the middle finger, and then jump back over. I liked this man. When the spy drone was flying over us for the tenth time, he asked us if we wanted him to throw a shovel at it. We said, "Please don't, good sir," and kept on with the interview. He told us that he'll also sometimes distract the border agents with his shenanigans so that people can cross over without being noticed. Not every field experience is that dramatic, and once Covid hit we were shooting segments in our apartments, and no one in America was going to Mexico. Well, some people were, but that's not my business.

I worked with Trevor for five years, and people were always asking me how I felt about him leaving. I was sad to see him go but happy to see him leave, if that makes sense. He was ready after seven years, and I can understand that. He wanted to see what the next chapter of his life would be. He's a multimillionaire who can walk up to any woman in the street and get her number. He is doing all right. It was very weird having him gone, though. Leslie Jones, Wanda Sykes, Chelsea Handler, and all the guest hosts were great, but at first it was a little bit like being a kid and your favorite teacher goes on maternity leave all of a sudden and you have a sub the rest of the year. Like, who is this person? They are nice and doing great, but at the end of the day you're like, *Where is Mrs. Wilson? She and her husband made a miracle and now I have this stranger in the class. I signed up for Mrs. Wilson's class! This is some trash!*

Chelsea Handler was the only guest host I really knew, and it was cool seeing people who had experience hosting shows do their thing. Marlon Wayans was a fun host who also happens to be a very attractive man. He was fine, but also so sweet, so I enjoyed that week very much. Wanda was very low-key, and

Leslie was very much involved from day one. I learned a lot watching each guest host—their different styles of comedy, how they integrate their style into the writing of the show, and the way they introduced their writing into the show. It also allowed me to showcase my talent to comedians that I respect and to show them how I work. They were all good, but they weren't Mrs. Wilson.

By the end of 2019, New York City was really taking a toll on me and I was very unhappy. More than ever, I was ready to go. When my contract was up in early 2020, right as the pandemic shut everything down, Reg was like, "Dulcé, there are no jobs, anywhere, at all. No clubs, no shows, no movies." So I signed a new contract. What else was I going to do? I couldn't even leave the house. They wanted a two-year extension, so I said one year. They said eighteen months, and I said one year and four months, until Reg said, "Just sign the two-year contract. It's only a difference of six months." Six months is a long time. But it's an even longer time in a pandemic with no job.

I was supposed to leave in July 2022, but then I realized something very important—I wanted to buy my mom a house. And that house was going to be in LA, so I needed to save up some more money if I was going to buy us our dream home. And the only way to do that was to talk to the boss man. So I called Trevor, the boss man aka Mrs. Wilson. I asked if I could stay until the end of December 2022 to save up some more money for a down payment and . . . he said yes. Yay! Then the network asked me to stay two more years, but I stuck to my guns and said no. So the end of December 2022 became the date. But then Trevor quit in September. Oh, shit. Did I just lose my job? Oh, shit. What am I gonna do? Oh, I still have a job. Thank God. Wait . . . who is going to host? Oh, he is hosting until the end of the year. Oh, then we can leave at the same time. Look at God! But then Comedy Central called again and asked me to stay until the end of March 2023. They knew I wasn't going to do another year. And I wasn't, but I did a pre-application for a home loan and they said I didn't have enough credit (who knew that was a fucking thing). So I couldn't get the house, and more money for a down payment wouldn't hurt. I said yes to the contract. Then they offered to make me a contributor until the end of the year. Sounds amazing. But when was I going to get to host a week? I found out my hosting week was the first week of May, so they extended my extension to my hosting week and THEN I would be a contributor and could move to LA. If this was exhausting to read, imagine how I felt living it.

When I told my mom I was moving back to Los Angeles, she said, "Great—I'll come with you!" It wasn't the plan for my mom to come with me immediately. But next thing you know, even her German shepherd and my brother were packing and getting one-way tickets. So now I needed to have enough money for a down payment on a house in LA for me *and* my mom and my brother and a cat and a dog. Yes, my mother has a dog. A fucking German shepherd. My mother has a K-9 unit, Civil

Rights—era, attacking people—ass dog. Anyway, I didn't sleep well in New York, so I wanted a real house that would finally feel like a home, even with a German shepherd in it. New York took a toll on my body, mind, and spirit, and even though leaving the friends I'd made was bittersweet, I got on that plane for the next adventure that has become my life.

EIGHT

I'm Such a Fan!

S ome people dream of getting famous enough to get recognized in public, but those people have never had a strange woman charge them like an NFL linebacker on the streets of Manhattan. Or—even more terrifying than that—take the drunk forty-something-year-old white lady who came up to me at the Improv Atlanta one night after a show. She didn't charge me, but she did stumble over with a big, crooked smile on her face. This lady put her hand on my arm and leaned in, like she was about to share a government secret with me.

"You are sooooo, sooo funny . . . Holy shit, you're hilarious. . . ."

"Thank you, ma'am," I said. I thought that would be it. But you know what, friends? I was wrong.

"Kate!! Kate!! Doesn't she look just like Adelaide?!" This woman was not slurring at me in a soft, subtle tone. She was screaming so loud, everyone in the club could hear.

"Who is Adelaide?" I wanted Adelaide to be a friend of theirs. I really did.

"Adelaide is THE WOMAN WHO RAISED ME!"

Ugh! This bitch.

Kate did what any self-respecting citizen who is mortified by her racist best friend would do—she pretended she'd never laid eyes on her in her life. Then the woman's husband rushed over and grabbed her arm. "I am so sorry," he said to me, his head hanging low in shame. Didn't he know she was racist when he married her? Or did she just surprise him one day during their honeymoon dressed in full blackface yelling, "Look, honey! I got a tan!"

As he pulled her away, she kept on yelling. "She looks just like Adelaide!!! Just like her!"

It's nice to know that this lady still thinks about Adelaide, but that was some bullshit. Getting recognized can be flattering, but not when some white lady is telling you that you look like her Black nanny; that also means that to her, you look like every other Black woman she's come across. And if that's not enough bullshit to deal with, there are the people who think my hair is public property, so they feel just fine reaching over and touching my Afro without permission.

Asking to pat, rub, fondle, or tug my hair is rude, but not asking is something else. White women have stuck their hand straight through my hair, all the way down to my scalp, and then fluffed it around like I'm a poodle in the Westminster Dog Show. I did a bit about this on *Conan*, if you recall from chapter 6! That's my head you are messing with! My hair that I took time to do, and not so some stranger could go spelunking in there. I've learned to spot these people from forty feet away. I've perfected the duck-and-spin move when I feel them getting close, so I can get out of the way before their hands get anywhere near my body.

Run-ins with strangers can be startling, but when it comes to *dating* fans, I have made this mistake exactly once, with a cute Jewish guy in Canada. Now, I love Jewish men. They may be handsome, cultured, funny, and loyal, but the main reason I love Jewish men is because they are circumcised, which means I do not have to roll, fold, or organize their penis when we have sex. I had a show in Toronto a few years ago, and a cute Jewish dude came up to me afterward and started flirting, so I flirted back. We exchanged numbers and he asked me to dinner. Mind you, it was after a show, so we didn't go to dinner until one in the morning. That's how I learned that at Chinese restaurants in

Toronto, you can ask for "cold tea" to drink, which is code for ordering a cocktail. That seems like a very easy code to break. Like I didn't need a password to get in here. This place was very well lit, and there was no bouncer in sight. I think I actually saw a cop eating chow mein. I was still very excited to say the code. When I did, the server rolled his eyes, scoffed, and said, "Yeah, yeah. What do you want to drink?" *Sir! We are doing a thing! You have to follow the rules of your establishment.* I was very disappointed. The late-night drinking laws must be strict there, so the cold tea thing is a way for everyone to still get drunk without breaking the law. Or maybe it's just a way for people in Canada to feel sneaky and dangerous. Let me stop. I got my own business to mind.

As we waited for our seats, there was one of those big lobster tanks sitting at the front of the restaurant, with a bunch of live, depressed lobsters bobbing around inside, spending their last precious moments surrounded by a bunch of drunk humans. I watched one Middle Eastern dude who'd probably had too many cold teas take off his leather jacket, reach his bare arm into the tank, grab a lobster, hold it in the air, take a picture, and throw it back in. Somewhere on Instagram there is a photo of a drunk fool holding up a lobster in a Canadian Chinese food joint with his big, hairy arm. I remember watching this and thinking, *What is going on in this city?* I thought Canadians were supposed to be *better* than Americans, not worse.

After the lobster fiasco, I had a nice night and morning with this dude. Eventually it was time for me to go back to New York, though. Once I was home, we didn't really communicate. I didn't talk to him again until a year and a half later, when Covid hit. During lockdown we FaceTimed all the time, which was not strange at all, because everyone's relationships were happening through screens, unless they lived together, and most of those couples are divorced now. We talked all day or all night. He would call when he was alone, or with his friends, or . . . post-coitus. But I didn't know that. I thought I was just talking to my friend, and then I found out he was FaceTiming me *from another Black woman's house*. I discovered this when she sat down next to him and asked, "Who are you talking to?" Fair question, sis. And then we both asked why he was calling me after they just had sex. Before this, things were going okay with us, but then George Floyd was murdered. This dude put the black square on Instagram like many people did. But the next day he called me complaining that since he had posted the square he lost some of his 125 followers, so he took it down because he didn't want to offend people. When I got angry about all this, he said, "I don't want any problems with you today, Dulcé."

To which I replied: "Let me call you back."

I don't want to complain too much about having fans, because y'all are the reason I am writing this book (thank you). Still. Some of y'all have to calm down. Sometimes I want to lounge on a beautiful beach with my friends and just chill. It's hard to do that when a stranger runs over and starts jumping up and down, screaming my name. This doesn't happen all the time. I know I'm not Angela Bassett. But it does happen. Imagine a warm Miami beach. The sky is blue, the waves are crashing, and all I want to do is enjoy my Cadillac margarita with my homeboys and relax. And then:

"OH MY GOD!!! Can I get a picture? Where's my phone?? WHERE IS MY PHONE?!?!"

On that beautiful beach in Miami, a pretty Black girl was losing her fucking mind, breathing heavy and jumping up and down so fast I thought she might have a heart attack.

"OH MY GOD YOU'RE DULCÉ SLOAN!!"

This girl could not function.

"It's okay," I said. "You're fine. Just relax, girl. It is not that serious, friend."

"BUT . . . I LOVE YOU."

"Thank you, but you've got to chill."

As she screamed at her friends to find her phone, she told me she was there for her friend's bachelorette party. They were all looking cute, having their hot girl beach day. These were the girls who get into clubs and past the velvet rope for free, every time. So you can imagine the commotion I was dealing with.

"Don't move!" she yelled as she searched for her phone.

"Ma'am, I am not going anywhere," I said. I was lounging on a towel—where was I darting off to?

"Found it!!"

She ran back over and had one of her friends take a picture.

So somewhere on Instagram there is a photo of me trying to just chill on a Miami beach, standing with a pretty Black girl who is losing her mind.

What most people don't know is that when I meet people on the street, on a beach, or at an event, I'm actually afraid of disappointing them. Even doing "meet and greets" at clubs, where you say hello to audience members after the show, gets me worried. I don't do them as much as I used to. I understand you think you know me. You see me on TV or onstage or social media and see me talk about my life, and feel like you know me like a best friend. But . . . *I don't know you.* And sometimes it feels like people want me to match their energy when I meet them after a show, and then I feel like my reaction disappoints people. I'm excited and happy to have y'all come and see my shows because without y'all I might have to go back to selling stucco. My mom always tells me, "You should talk to everyone." But I hate to feel like I've disappointed somebody who paid money to see me onstage, or someone who bulldozes me at a beach. I promise, I am trying my best.

The racist and fat-phobic comments don't help the situation. Those are fun. People don't realize that Trevor would get death threats. *The Daily Show* pisses a lot of people off—usually people who don't like Black, Brown, Gay, Trans, Asian, or Female humans. This hostility can make you a little wary of people who sprint up to you on the street. Once someone sent me what looked like a greeting card from one of those mass-produced greeting card companies, but inside it was like:

Dear Miss Sloan,

You think you're so funny but really you're a . . .

I closed the card and didn't finish reading that racist nonsense. I turned it in to security because, yes, we have security for moments just like this. Maybe that's why I have my guard up when I'm walking through the Milwaukee airport and some woman with big NPR tote-bag energy rushes up and says, "Can I give you a joke for *The Daily Show?*"

"No thank you."

"But it's really funny and you don't have to credit me or pay for it."

"Oh, you don't have to worry about that. Because no thank you. Have a great day."

Now, what do you think my answer to that should be? What would *you* do if some Terry Gross look-alike ran up to you in an airport? And I love Terry Gross. I was more disappointed than they were. If it WAS Terry, that's one thing, but imagine it's not. Imagine it's some lady with her tote and her crazy eyes, asking if she can pitch a joke. You would think she'd lost her damn mind. You would be scared! You would say, "Excuse me, but no. No you cannot." And let me tell you how many people I have come across who are not at all used to hearing the word NO. Y'all need to learn to take rejection with the grace of a comic. Please.

Again, I am not bashing fans. I love (most of) y'all.

I might not go up to people I admire and run my hand through their hair or ask them if I can give them acting advice, even though they have an Oscar. But I can become a bumbling fan and make a fool of myself. When I met Angela Bassett, I lost my damn mind. She was just standing there, like a gorgeous goddess from heaven. I did a desk piece on the show that day and she saw it! When she was coming up to the stage for her interview, she walked up to me, SHE TOOK MY HANDS IN HER HANDS (yes they were soft and of course she smelled good), and said, "You are so funny and talented."

What. Was. HAPPENING!!!!!

My brain was like . . . what is happening right now?? Is Miss Angela Evelyn Bassett gazing into my eyes, telling me I am amazing and talented, and holding my hand in her hand? She was. SHE WAS, friends! I don't even think I was speaking English to her, I was so flustered. And do you know what I said back to her? Did I casually thank her and tell her to have fun on the show? Did I strike up a deep conversation about acting techniques or ask her about her husband, who she always calls by his full name, Courtney B. Vance? No. I said, "I'm so sorry, Angela Bassett, but I might faint right now and take you down with me." She looked at the makeup artist and wardrobe head to confirm this. And they nodded. She turned back to me and slowly pulled her hands away. I dropped my head slightly and said, "I'm sorry." And she left to do her interview.

That was July 29, 2019. After she'd done her interview with

Trevor, she walked by and said, in her beautiful Angela Bassett voice, "You all right now?"

"Yes, ma'am. Thank you."

I never get starstruck, but something happens to the planets and the space-time continuum when Angela Bassett holds your hand, I swear. Not a day went by that I didn't think about correcting my behavior and showing her I was cool, relaxed, and not a crazed fan.

Besides that first meeting with Angela (can I call her Angela now?), the only other time I freak out is when I meet a drag queen I love. When I did a guest-hosting spot on *RuPaul's Drag Race*, I was a blubbering idiot. My career was still at a point where I had to beg my agents to get a producer to put me on the show. They brought me on for a few days to help the queens do a comedy roast of Ross Mathews. I got way more emotional than I thought I would when I was thanking RuPaul for letting my dream of being a guest judge on the show come true. I was kind of crying, so who knows what she thought of me. At least I didn't faint.

I have met so many amazing queens from the world of *RuPaul's Drag Race*. Bob the Drag Queen, Jinkx Monsoon, Brita Filter, Kerri Colby, and so many others. I should keep pictures of them on me like trading cards. My biggest fangirl moment was with Miss Congeniality herself, Nina West. I was at the Emmys in 2018 and she came up to me and took my hand just like Angela had. This time, though, the feeling was mutual. We were holding hands, freaking out, saying, "Oh my God, I love you!!" Our conversation went like this:

Nina: "You're the best!"

Me: "No, you're the best!"

Nina: "No, you are the best!"

Me: "I'm a huge fan!"

Nina: "No, I'm a huge fan!"

Me: "You're amazing!"

Nina: "No, you're amazing!"

Me: "Sorry I'm being weird!"

Nina: "Sorry I'M being weird!!"

Now this was a good fan interaction because we were on the same page. Same energy. Neither of us knew how to act, so we were both embarrassing ourselves and it worked out great. After our moment together, we went our separate ways, and unlike with Angela, I have no regrets.

Like I said, not many famous people would freak me out, and I don't want someone freaking out about me. Only Angela Bassett, Nina West, and maybe Carol Burnett could make me lose all sense. Oh, and Jane fucking Fonda. Bro, Jane has some serious movie-star vortex energy, and I have felt it in the flesh.

When I did the Amazon show *Yearly Departed*, it was me, X Mayo, Meg Stalter, Chelsea Peretti, Aparna Nancherla, Yvonne Orji, and . . . Jane fucking Fonda. Yvonne Orji was the host. The show is a roast of the year that's ending, so we got to take down 2021 and talk shit about all the messed-up things that happened throughout the year. We were all sitting in this mock-up of a church with stained glass windows and a pulpit, like we were at a funeral. We'd all met and rehearsed and done our bits at the podium, so we were sitting in the pews, facing forward. The double doors were open behind us, and we could not see who was entering since we don't have eyes in the back of our heads like parents and first grade teachers do. But this *feeling* came into the room. We all looked at each other like, "Yo, who the fuck is here?" My friend X Mayo looked at me.

"What *is* that?"

We all felt it. When we turned around to look, there was Jane Seymour Fonda, just standing there with her energy, or whatever it was, radiating out from her. She does her part at the pulpit and then leaves, unlike the rest of us, because she had earned the right to not sit on set all day. When she says goodbye to everyone and graciously thanks us for all our YOU ARE JANE FUCKING FONDA energy, she looks at me and says, "I know you! You do such great work." And, friends, she gives me a hug. "I watch you every night," she tells me.

She floated down the aisle and out the double doors. I was stunned. I turned to X Mayo, still in shock.

"How does Jane Fonda know who I am? I'm just li'l ol' me."

"Dude, you're on TV," X Mayo reminds me.

"Oh yeah, that makes sense."

I guess I am on TV, but that does not mean I will not fangirl out when the legend that is Jane Fonda enters a room.

I know y'all are hoping and praying that I got a chance to meet Angela Bassett again. Well . . . I did! Ahhhhhhhh! It was February 24, 2023. The Lord himself blessed me with the opportunity to redeem myself. I was at the dinner for the NAACP Awards hanging out in the Moët Hennessy Award winners lounge (yes, you read that right), drinking Moët from a gold chalice, when I hear, "Clear the way for Angela Bassett." This was my chance! I put down my chalice and I stood right near the path they were clearing. When she walked in she looked right at me and said, "Hi, how are you?" And she had the biggest smile on her face. I guess she was glad that I didn't faint. I walked over to her.

"I'm so glad to see you, Miss Angela Bassett. I have to redeem myself for the last time we met when I said I was gonna faint."

She just smiled and shook her head and said, "You are so funny."

She went and took a picture with the cast of the show *Harlem*, who had just won their awards (congratulations!), and security was clearing a path for her to leave. I stood near the path again and asked for a photo, and she said yes. I think I am the only person in that lounge she took a picture with who wasn't holding an award. That picture was my reward! I did it!

NINE

Not Today, Sir!

The Civil Rights Museum in Memphis, Tennessee, is attached to the Lorraine Motel. That's where Martin Luther King Jr. was assassinated, for those who don't pay attention to history. I was in town for the Memphis Comedy Festival in 2019, and part of the deal was that the performers got free tickets to the museum. I would have paid, but they were handing them out, so who was I to say no. I was there with my friend Peggy, an Irish American comedian from Pennsylvania.

Our tour guide that day was a nice Black man who was a retired public school teacher. Now, I love public school teachers, but you might remember that I also have loved to question them since I was that little girl moving back and forth between Miami and Atlanta. The tour guide starts talking about the transatlantic slave trade and telling all the folks on the tour that Black people were not enslaved in America for four hundred years. He had to say it more than once because many people in the crowd were pondering everything they had ever been taught.

"You see, the first West Africans were brought to America and enslaved in 1619. Make sure you say 'enslaved.' It was an atrocity that happened to them. They didn't come over as slaves like it was an occupation. Now, the Emancipation Proclamation was signed in 1863, and the last enslaved people were freed in Texas in June 1865, so that would be 246 years, not four hundred."

He took folks out with that big fact! Why is everybody running around throwing out four hundred years? When my teachers in school told this same story, I questioned them, too. I have been correcting people for years. If it was four hundred years ago, that means slavery in America started in 1465. That's twenty-seven years before Columbus's ol' goofy ass hopped on them three ships and destroyed the Western Hemisphere. The four-hundred-years-ago thing is in the Bible, bro. It's not us!

At the museum, you do things like sit in the hold of a slave ship to get an idea of what the Middle Passage was like. You also watch a locally produced movie about Black history. It goes through the experiences of our ancestors into the current day, inspiring hope for the future. They did a good job. From there the movie screen slides back and you walk right into the Jim Crow exhibit. Did you know there were more Black congressmen in America during Reconstruction than there are now? One of the first suburbs was in New Jersey, and Black folks were not allowed. Anyway, Peggy and I were listening to the guide and looking around, but we started talking about the most recent congressman sex scandal.

Peggy leaned over to me and whispered, "He did WHAT?!"

It took about half a second for someone in the group to shush us. Now, please know, if there is anything that runs through me, it is being aggressively shushed. I am not in elementary school. And even then I didn't appreciate an aggressive shushing.

I turned my head to see who had the nerve and the gall to shush another adult who pays taxes, and I saw a white man old enough to remember when the Reverend Dr. Martin Luther King Jr. was alive. This motherfucker shushed us?! I'm sorry. What? I'm about five feet four inches tall and the old man is over six feet tall. Right behind him there was a backlit display of a Klan uniform that was raised up so it was about eight feet high, making it look like the ghost of a Klansman was hovering behind this man.

"Sir, this is not the place to be shushing Black people," I said very sternly.

"I can't hear," he said, with his ancestor, the Klansman, hovering behind.

"Then you need to move closer." And he did. And I'm glad he did because there was way too much fucking symbolism for me in that moment.

Did he not realize I was experiencing Jim Crow in real time? For the rest of the tour, the old white man stayed as far away from me and Peg as he could. That was fine by me. Later we saw the Rosa Parks bus exhibit, which is a re-creation of the bus Rosa Parks was on when she refused to give up her seat. There was a tour guide specifically for this exhibit. She asked all of us to take a seat and she explained what Rosa Parks did that day and she talked about the Montgomery bus boycott. There was a statue of Rosa in one of the seats, to re-create the scene to make us feel like we were living and breathing history. At the end of her speech the tour guide pointed at me and said, "And Rosa sat in that seat right there." My seat? This seat? What? My question was, why didn't they put the Rosa statue in her seat? Do they *want* people to take her seat? We all got up and I told Peg that the history was getting too real. I just had a showdown with a Klansman and then had to start a bus boycott. I didn't know what to do in 2018, so what would I have done in 1955?

If I sound like I didn't like the museum, I didn't—I loved it. It was a lot to take in, and it was designed that way, because Black

Americans have been through pure hell. But overall, it was a great day. There were photos of a young, handsome Ambassador Andrew Young looking pissed. I would look aggravated all the time, too, if my job was to protect Martin Luther King Jr. Have you ever tried to keep someone from getting assassinated? Me neither. The last stop on the tour was the actual hotel room that Martin Luther King Jr. was staying in when he was murdered. The museum connects to the Lorraine Motel, and they kept his room just as it was, like a time capsule. There's cigarettes in the ashtray, the phone is off the hook. There's a memorial wreath to commemorate his death, but that's about the only change. When you step out the door of the hotel room, you're standing in the spot where he was murdered. It was so emotional, I finally understood the Rosa Parks statue not being in her seat. I did not, however, forgive the shusher. Y'all need to stop telling Black women to be quiet, especially if you are standing in front of an eight-foot-tall Klan uniform.

It was a long day, and it was interesting to watch my white comedian friends interact with the museum. Adam, a young white comic from Indiana who came down for the festival, told me they didn't teach any of the history in the museum at his school. He didn't know about Black kids being sprayed with firehoses or attacked by dogs. He was a baby when 9/11 happened, but STILL. He was distraught, like he'd just learned that Santa isn't real and human beings are monsters.

But as a comic and a Black person, my brain has a default

that keeps me from getting too overwhelmed and sad in certain situations. So me and my homeboy David, who is a young Black comic from Atlanta, were looking at all the exhibits about segregation and couldn't help but wonder things like: Were strip clubs ever segregated? Were Black women having "pole-ins" at white strip clubs? Refusing to stop "shaking that thang" until the cops showed up? Milkshakes were being poured over the heads of Black students at lunch counters to break their spirits, but that doesn't work with strippers. What are you going to do? Pour champagne on them? Did Black women invent the champagne shower? I'm not saying having these conversations was right; I'm saying we had to do it so we didn't burst into tears. Adam was watching the footage of the student sit-ins and repeating, "I can't believe we did this. . . . I can't believe we did this. . . ."

Me and the older Black people surrounding him were like, "Yup, and welcome to the world, sir." It reminds me of the night Donald Trump was elected president and one of my straight white male friends called me crying like a baby. He's from a small town in Washington State, so everyone he knew growing up was white.

"I can't believe this," he sobbed over the phone. "I didn't know America was so racist!"

Excuse me again, but—where the fuck have you been? That election gave us a color-coded map of racism in America. It'll always be interesting the way white people are confused about America. They're like, "Why are Black people not afraid of

Trump?" Well, because our mothers have been telling us there was an evil white man coming, so we were not at all surprised. Plus we've met this same man as a cop, a teacher, a grocery clerk with attitude. Trump is just the one with the microphone who says the quiet parts loud. If the Republican Party could stop being racist for fifteen minutes and realize how many Black and brown conservatives are out there, they would win every election. But since most of them are probably not reading this book unless they're reading it just so they can send me some hate mail in the form of a greeting card (hello, sir), they'll probably never take their fifteen-minute break from being who they truly are.

I still stand by the idea that my comedy is not political, even though I can go off (see above) when needed. People ask if my stand-up is a form of resistance, and to that I say, I am talking about dicks, bro. I'm talking about being single and learning to stay away from broke men. The very act of me doing stand-up is seen as a political act, but really, can't I just talk about men's penises and be left alone?

One of those times that I needed to go off also happened in 2019, at the LBJ Library's Summit on Race in Texas. I was asked to be on a panel with George Lopez, Sasheer Zamata, and Aparna Nancherla. There was an older white man moderator who was about as funny as a death certificate. The whole audience as far as my eyes could see was full of white people. At one point, the moderator started asking us about our contributions to the entertainment industry. He didn't mean box office or awards; he meant how had our presence changed the culture or some bullshit. Well, I could not help myself. I told this man that every form of entertainment had been stolen from us. We started it all, and we keep creating new things that get stolen again, and then we're asked about our "contributions" as if we were just getting started. Bro, please. We have been contributing to America the entire time!

Once I went off, the whole audience started clapping, like I was saying something they'd never thought of or heard in their entire lives. At one point I was like, how are you having a seminar on race, and the only people of color are on this stage? George Lopez grabbed my hand, partly out of solidarity and partly because he may have seen I was getting heated and about to blow up. He said, "Y'all need to listen to her." I was so frustrated by what was happening. It was like they were asking us to prove our worth, but they have no idea what experiences Black and brown people go through. I started talking about growing up in a Latin neighborhood in Atlanta, and the fact that when I was nineteen years old I watched ICE come in on a Sunday morning and grab neighbors and whole families out of their homes and deport them. I counted eight twenty-passenger vans full of people taken away. Whole apartment buildings were empty in a matter of minutes. I was looking out the window during the raid and an ICE agent walked by, looked me in the face, and said out loud to himself, "Not her."

These people went to work every day. Contributed to the

American economy. Just like my ancestors did. So yeah, I was pissed as I sat on that stage. It is not my job to teach a bunch of paying white folks what racism looks like. Again after I said all this, people started clapping. I told them to stop.

"Quit clapping, y'all."

And then they'd clap louder.

"Well, y'all paid me already, so I can say what I want."

I could feel the moderator's tension from across the stage. It only made me want to go harder, so I went OFF on that crowd. I wish I could tell you what I said, but I truly don't remember because I was mad as shit. The other panelists watched quietly and nodded their heads while I made sure the audience knew that we were not there to teach them anything, and it was not our damn job to make them better citizens. And you know what? When I was finished, they clapped some more.

The best part of that whole experience was that Andrew Young himself was there, watching. He was a very handsome man back in the 1960s when he was one of the top lieutenants for Dr. King, and so when he came up to me after the event, shook my hand, and said, "Young lady, everything you said up there was great," I almost passed out in front of him. In all the photos I'd seen of him back in the day, he was looking fine, being annoyed, arms crossed and eyes scanning for danger. The man had good reason to be fucking agitated. No one was smiling while they marched on Selma. I decided to show Andrew Young my homeboy's Instagram Story, because he'd posted photos of Mr. Young from the Civil Rights Museum, looking concerned, mad, or annoyed. I was showing the series of photos and he stopped me.

"Do you want me to tell you the story behind this photo?" Mr. Young said.

"Yes, sir, I absolutely do."

In the photo, Mr. Young was standing there in a nice, long leather jacket, looking pissed next to Dr. King in front of a group of people. In the photo, an old white man holding a clipboard is talking to him.

"That man was telling us that there were some cracker shooters in the bushes who wanted to shoot the Reverend. He said, 'They are gonna shoot the one in the suit.'"

Mr. Young said that to confuse the shooters, he told everyone to dress in the same suit as Dr. King so they wouldn't know which Black man to kill, since every Black man looked alike to them anyway.

"I did it so they couldn't figure out who to kill," he said.

DAMN.

The museum plaque didn't say anything about all that. I got the real story, from the man himself.

"You want to take a picture?" Mr. Young asked.

"Yes, sir!" I exclaimed. He was sitting in an electric wheelchair since he's an older gentleman, and I was standing, so he put his arm around my waist. I couldn't smile big enough. A civil rights icon and former mayor of Atlanta just complimented me about going off on a room full of white folks?! Did I forget to mention that I was at this event the week following my trip to the Civil Rights Museum? Talk about full circle. Taking a photo with Ambassador Young is every Atlanta child's dream. He is the reason I can pee where I want, eat where I want, and yell at whoever I please. I would have let him motorboat me if he wanted to. He's the reason I can vote! Come on, y'all!

TEN

Self-Care— Who Is She?

Theres's a phrase I learned in church as a kid: *Favor ain't fair.* God raises some people up, and lets others work at Value City and do local dinner theater their whole life. I did both of those things, so no disrespect. I have been blessed as hell with my career (thank you, Lord), but does that make me

worthy of writing a memoir? What do I have to teach? I'm not
Michelle Obama or Viola Davis. I am still figuring my shit out,
but here we are.

For every celebrity you see, whether they're in comedy, acting,
sports, or they're a famous tech bro, there are thousands of
other people who are working to get exactly where they are. I
know so many talented comedians and actors who cannot catch
a break, and no one knows why some people make it and then
write books, and others—who are talented as hell—never get
the opportunity. I'm not talking about the no-talent fools. But
the talented ones out there, I cannot figure out the mystery of
why they don't get that favor. I guess like the pastor said, *It's not
fair*. All I know is you better do all you can to make sure you're
the one getting the favor. That's not always so easy.

When it comes to my career, I feel pretty positive. There is
always more I want to do. I already mentioned my dream of
playing a Klingon on *Star Trek*, but I would love to do Broadway.
I have been missing doing theater a lot. The last time I was in
a play was 2010. I want to do fantasy like *Game of Thrones*, and
I want to work with the Muppets.

But what stresses me out and keeps me up until four in the
morning is my personal life. I am about to turn forty years old.
By the time you read this I'll be barreling toward forty-one. I go
to bed alone, and I wake up alone. I have never been more single
than I was in New York, which is part of the reason I needed to
get out of there. What is wrong with New York men? We asked

y'all to stop catcalling and harassing us on the street, we didn't ask for radio silence.

I'm thankful that I have a successful career, but that's half of my life. In America, people think that as long as you're happy with your job and you're making money, you should be completely happy. And I am, I am. But . . . sometimes I feel like I am waiting to be a whole person, waiting for a man, waiting for a baby. I was telling all this to one of my homegirls, and instead of feeling sorry for me, she said, "Maybe you'll stop feeling so bad about things when you stop thinking you're living half a life." But that is hard because for women it is two different things. We are always asked to make a choice between a career or a family, while a man is never asked the same thing. As if they don't work and have families, too.

I'm a Black Southern woman. Most of us don't learn self-care growing up. Everybody else comes before we do—our kids, teachers, friends, elders, aunties, uncles, even the UPS guy. Our self-care is making sure our hair and nails are done, but that's about it. We are taught to take a recharge at a spa or take a trip with our girls. But a "mental health day"? Who is she? Who her mama 'nem? We have people to feed and bills to pay. I did not learn about self-care until . . . now. It only took me forty years. My mom taught me how to survive, but she didn't teach me how to process stress, because she wasn't taught that. She taught me not to let anyone disrespect me, but self-love? In the South, that was some granola, no-shoes-wearing bullshit.

When I was growing up, my mom would do her own nails and hair, but besides that I don't remember her indulging in anything that *Vogue* would call self-care. If you went to church on Sundays and your family was fed and doing fine, there was no room for complaining. She did sometimes pick us up after school on a Friday in Atlanta and drive us twelve hours to go see my grandma in Miami. Then we'd turn around on Sunday and drive back. I never understood why she would drive twenty-four hours in a forty-eight-hour time period with two kids in the car until recently. It's crazy to drive that far for anything, but there must have been a reason. It took me a while to figure it out, but I think that sometimes, you just need to see your mom. That was her form of self-care. That's what she had.

Besides taking care of her hair and nails and going on marathon road trips, my mom did quit smoking cold turkey when I was about fourteen years old. She lost weight and started eating healthy. She took care of herself in that way, and she was protective of us, and that made me protective of her from a young age. I put my mom, my brother, my cousins, and friends first, but taking care of myself? Friends, that was not happening unless my mom was doing my nails or we were going shopping for pleather outfits at your local Simply Fashions or Rainbow. I still love Rainbow. If you see me on TV and I'm NOT on *The Daily Show*, ya girl is probably in head-to-toe Rainbow. Looking good and flammable. I was doing an episode of *Comedy Knockout*, and the wardrobe head popped in my dressing room and asked, "Do you want me to steam your clothes?"

"Girl, no. They will melt. I can't wear this shirt near a hot cup of tea."

We all know that I am exaggerating (I'm not finna let Rainbow sue me. Shit).

When my mom got older, she started going to high tea. We would go to nice hotels or have it at Château Élan after a pedicure. The little sandwiches and pretty teacups made her feel good, like she was indulging in something just because *it was fun*. It wasn't about anybody else but her. Then she created "Majestic Meals." This was right after I finished college. She'd set up a fancy enclosed green tent, and she'd print up pretty menus with things like lamb sausage with dates, curry chicken, and cakes. She would set up the tent with a beautiful table setting, nice cushions for the chairs, fancy tablecloths, and three-tiered serving trays. She would bring out a pretty tea box so me and whoever else was there—cousins, friends—could pick out our tea flavor. I loved the African Rooibos. We were on the patio of our Norcross apartment complex, but we would be transported to a completely different place. Someone would drive by blasting Norteño music, but in our minds we were at a fancy garden party at a palatial estate.

After years of working, paying bills, and looking out for everyone else but me, it's about damn time I figured out my own version of Majestic Meals. I have been working since I was a kid. You're at the end of this not-a-memoir, so you know how many jobs I've had. I am grateful for every success I've had, but I am TIRED. When I finally froze my eggs as a backup plan because I will be having kids when I'm in my forties, I started to feel it. When you freeze your eggs, you do what's called a retrieval, where the doctor takes out any eggs you have after all the shots and hormones work their magic. You might start with twelve eggs on that first day, but then eight eggs might mature. Of those, maybe two will be what they call viable. It is not for the fainthearted, friends, and maybe you can see why going through it made me depressed.

I try to take care of myself, and I am afraid of drugs. You know the D.A.R.E. program, the campaign to keep kids off drugs? Most people thought the ads where they fried an egg and told you that's what your brain looked like on drugs were stupid. But me? That shit terrified me. I don't drink a lot, because I don't like being drunk. I don't like the feeling of not being in control. When I was in college, I was the one making sure my friends didn't end up in a Lifetime movie, so I had to stay alert. Tipsy, yes. Blackout drunk? Never. Who is gonna make sure LeeAnne doesn't lose her scholarship?

Before I froze my eggs, I was depressed. I mean very depressed. But I wouldn't say it out loud. I finally told my mom what was going on, and she told me something that surprised me.

"When I was your age, I got depressed, too," she said. I knew she worked hard and put everyone else first—besides her pedicures and Majestic Meals. Then I remembered a time when she would come home from work and go into her room for a few hours. I thought she just had a long day at work, but she told me she was depressed.

"I think my mother was depressed, too," she said. So it's a whole lineage of being down. My mom went through Jim Crow. The first time she went to school with white people, she was ten years old. My grandma was born during the Depression, and my grandfather was born in 1913, the youngest of thirteen children. My great-grandparents were born in the 1800s, so what I am saying is I am not that far removed from Reconstruction. I have a lot of guilt for feeling depressed! Look at what the people before me went through, and how dare I complain and feel sad?! The nerve of me. But studies have proven that trauma can be passed down genetically. So pair that with the fact that I am very hard on myself, and I never learned to put myself first, and you get a sad lady who is worn the fuck out. But this time, I am not feeling guilty or apologizing, and neither should you.

I had a lot of hang-ups about going to therapy, because telling a stranger my business is not how I was raised. I'll tell my cousins, friends, and hairdresser, but someone holding a clipboard who I do not know? That was too much. And then paying them? I was told that was some white people shit. Like kissing a dog on the mouth or talking back to your parents. I didn't know any people of color growing up who didn't say that was white people shit. After hearing me sound sad on the phone too many times, my manager, Reg, started telling me to try therapy. He had to tell me a lot, though, because like I said—I had hang-ups. My grandparents didn't go to therapy, so how dare I do it?

"Just try it," Reg would say. I would always say maybe, but then never do anything about it.

"I know you're tired of telling me to go," I said one day after he'd asked me for the umpteenth time.

"I'm not tired of telling you. I will always tell you. I'm tired of you not going."

Oh.

For some reason, that was what I needed to hear. I don't know why or what it was, but after that I started looking for a therapist.

Whatever I was doing (or not doing) wasn't helping. I wasn't feeling any better, so maybe he had a point. So I finally broke and started therapy. Now I'm working on learning boundaries, giving myself grace, speaking to myself in a nicer way. I'm working on looking at my situation as a positive one, instead of one where I wake up hating my life. I am learning that if someone hurts me and I choose not to speak to them for six months, that is not me being a bitch or causing harm, it is me creating a boundary.

I'm sorry, what?!? There has been a name for this all this time? Me giving somebody the coldest shoulder ever was all a part of me healing?!? Ohhhh, bitch! Y'all done fucked up now. They should never let ME learn about boundaries!

My friend Josh Johnson says I am the only person who can make therapy sound like a threat. What do you mean, sir? I'm a delicate flower just trying to protect my peace. I am not fucking around anymore. I've always had a policy of icing out people who have hurt me, but now I have psychology to back it up. (Now imagine the "The more you know" logo flying by.)

Like I said, I hated the idea of therapy, but now my friends say I'm less reactionary, and I feel calmer. Everybody calls Black women angry, but nobody ever asks us why we're mad. No one goes, "You're raging inside? What happened?" They just think we're all walking around pissed, like we think it's fun. It's not fucking fun! It's exhausting. I didn't just pop out of the womb upset. We are at the mercy of everyone all the time. We spend our whole lives putting our hands in the air going, "I didn't do it!" We're perceived as aggressive, but we just need some self-care, some respect, and someone to say, "Hey, we see why you're angry, now go sit on the beach with a fruit drink and take care of yourself." Nobody does that for us, so we have to do it for ourselves.

I am not condoning woe-is-me whining and pampering yourself because you think the Illuminati are out there trying to keep you down. There are not a bunch of rich people sitting in a room plotting out ways to keep you poor. Beyoncé is busy! You think Jay Z is trying to make sure you stay in your old Camry? No, friend! He's busy, too. The roomful of people sitting in the congressional chamber trying to keep you poor is Congress. Go vote. If you're going to be angry at somebody, be angry at Congress, not the Carters. They want your money for concert tickets, not taxes. Go fucking vote. You can know the names of all the Housewives, but you should know who your senators are, too.

I have two friends, one in Atlanta and one in Los Angeles. Each of these friends, at different times, told me the same thing: if someone spoke to me the way I speak to myself, they'd fight them. What they meant was that the way we talk to ourselves matters. The longest relationship you'll have is the one with yourself, and it is so hard sometimes to be nice to yourself. So watch how you talk about yourself *to* yourself. Also, if something doesn't feel right (a relationship, a job)—it's not! Thanks to my therapist for that one. I can't fix anyone, especially a man. I have never tried to change a man, because that is not my responsibility. If he needs to change, then he will do it or he won't. And that goes for anyone. They better come to me fully fixed. Are you a trained professional? I'm not. If you are not in the mental health industry, you are not trained to make a man a better person. Let him GO. He will take you down, every time.

Women are wired to take care of another living being, sometimes to our detriment. I want to take care of another living being, but I want that person to be my own tiny infant baby, not some grown-ass man. I'm trying to take pressure off myself to have a family by the time I'm forty, because we are past that, friends. I'm trying not to be bogged down by this biological clock that started ticking when I was six years old. I'm also trying not to be bogged down by men who don't respect me. No more broke dick, and no more bullshit.

If you've ever used a stove, and I know you have, you have

burned yourself at least one time. So you can either put on oven mitts the next time you cook, or keep doing what you're doing, flipping pancakes with no spatula, and scalding your hand because you're being careless and don't want to learn a lesson. You can't blame the stove. That stove is not going to turn into a refrigerator, no matter how much you wish for it. You have to protect yourself, take care of yourself, put on a damn oven mitt.

I am not trying to write a memoir, and I am not trying to teach you how to cook. I am trying to figure out my next moves, my next steps. By the time you read this, I hope to be married and expecting my first child. I'm going to believe it and receive it. I'm going to give myself grace. I'm going to continue to speak nicer to myself. I'm going to change the mindset that makes me put what other people need before myself. I'm going to stop using helping others as a distraction from focusing on me. I'm going to do something every day to express love to myself. And y'all are gonna do the same. I'm not about to go through all this growth and healing by myself! Y'all betta come on. And the first step is—block their number. You were looking for a sign, well, this is a blaring neon sign out your window:

DO IT! I CAN SEE YOU!

Spilling the Tea in Quakertown

There you have it, friends. All my stories of dating, destiny, and day jobs. Tales of my youth, of road trips in the Deep South, of getting shushed at the Civil Rights Museum (no thank you, sir), and of becoming the performer I was destined to be.

I have spilled the tea, but not *all* the tea just yet. I have one final saga to share, and it'll prove that I was meant to be onstage, even if that stage is slippery as hell and I was cast as a bird in not one but FIVE shows. That's a lot of squawking.

Let me explain. The summer between my junior and senior year of college, I did a summer stock theater program in Quakertown, Pennsylvania—a town so small their Walmart Supercenter closed at 11 p.m. That might seem fine if you're a Yankee and you live in Quakertown, but disrespecting a Walmart is a sin to a Southerner. We all know that you can buy clothes, makeup, home decor, lawn chairs, Windex, sponges, plus you can send a FedEx, buy your groceries, and get your glasses fixed *at the same damn time*. When I found out the Walmart in Quakertown closed at 11 p.m., I knew that I and my fellow actors would have to find other ways to entertain ourselves. One of those ways would become GOSSIP. And let me tell you that tea was served piping hot on a regular basis, honey! Oh, it was divine.

To get this summer stock spot I had to audition against thousands of other theater kids at SETC, the Southeastern Theater Conference. Then I had to pray I got picked. That year's conference was in one of my favorite places in the world—wait for it—Chattanooga, Tennessee. Why, you ask? Chattanooga is only an hour and a half drive from Atlanta, and we all grew up going there on day trips with our friends or family. It's also the first place a lot of us "went out of town" with a significant other. There is Lookout Mountain, where they say you can see different states. (I don't know if that's true, since state lines are man-made, but it sounds cool.)

There is Rock City, and my favorite place, the Tennessee

Aquarium. It had salt- and freshwater fish displays, so half the aquarium was a gorgeous, vibrant blue with beautiful, colorful fish, and the other half was brown and tan with brown and tan fish because nature also has good and bad neighborhoods. My mom would take us all the time as kids. My favorite trip was when they had a catfish exhibit and my mom and some country white man spent the day plotting on the fish.

"It costs how much to get in here?!" my mom exclaimed. "For these prices I better get a meal at the end of this tour."

"Hell, I got some fishing poles in the truck! We can get this figured out," the country white man added.

"Everything in here would look good in hot grease and cornmeal."

"Just need some white bread and some mustard!"

They spent the rest of the day walking around laughing, asking employees if they could eat the fish and then telling them there should be a restaurant at the end of the tour where you can eat one of the fish you saw on display. It was hilarious. The employees didn't think so, but we had a great time. Remember the guy I dated who didn't know what an aquarium was? Well, he should probably take a trip to the Tennessee Aquarium. I mean he was right, though. It is technically a museum for fish.

So when you get your number for SETC, you find out if you're auditioning first or one thousandth. The sweet spot is to get something from 400 to 600. If you get lower numbers, that means some of the theater reps might not even be at the conference yet, since it's early days. Higher numbers mean that the reps have probably already chosen their actors and theater techs and left town. One good thing about my college theater program was that they would pay for us to attend the festival, cover our accommodations, and give us a $200 stipend. Otherwise there is no way I (or most of us) could have afforded it. They also had thespian celebrities at these events every year. At one conference, I got to meet Dawn Wells (aka Mary Ann on *Gilligan's Island*) and Terrence Mann. If you don't know who he is, he's a Tony-nominated Broadway actor who played Rum Tum Tugger in the original Broadway cast of *Cats!* This is a very big deal. The year before, he had actually asked me to audition for him just based off of me talking to him in passing at the conference. He was working with a production in North Carolina called *The Lost Colony* and EVERYBODY wanted that job. I didn't get it, maybe because I was super nervous when I auditioned. Or maybe it was fate and I wasn't supposed to spend a summer dressed as a dancing Native American.

The Chattanooga Hilton was definitely a step up from the Days Inn we had to stay at in country-ass Georgia in the fall of 2002. To get a number for SETC, you have to audition at the Georgia Theatre Conference. That year it was in Americus, Georgia. We drove through fields of cotton to get to that awful-ass hotel. Among all the stains and various broken or cracked items in the room, there was a used Band-Aid stuck to the curtains, just flapping in the wind. It was at such a height and angle that you knew someone had stuck it on the curtains intentionally. None of us would even sleep under the blankets. I didn't get picked that year, so the whole thing was a bust.

Each year at SETC, I would see this older white man who was the head of the lighting department at Disney World, and he would always check in on me. I was an actor-technician, meaning that I was an actor who had technical theater experience and I could use that experience to get a summer stock job. The whole goal was to be working at a theater any way you could. My freshman year of college I showed him my technical theater résumé and portfolio. I didn't have enough lighting experience to work for him at Disney World, but we had a great time talking, so we became buddies. Buddies who saw each other once every fifty-two weeks at that theater conference, but buddies nonetheless.

"Did you get a number this year?" he'd always ask.

"No, sir."

"Did you get any more lighting experience?"

"No, sir. I tried, but my school gives those opportunities to the technical theater students."

"Well, I would hire you if I could, but we both know you would rather be on the stage."

We never even remembered each other's names. It's funny how people just want to see that you're doing well, even if they barely know you. The year I got a number I made sure to find him to let him know.

"I got a number this year!"

"That's great! I knew you would! What is your number?"

"One thousand and one."

"The last day, huh?"

"Yeah."

"Well, that's great. You are gonna get a job. I just know it."

And he was right. And my actor-technician experience came in handy because that was how I got my first (and only) summer stock job.

The audition process is what is known as a "cattle call." Meaning they call literally 1,000-ish actors to come audition on the stage of a hotel ballroom for up to two or three minutes each. There are three categories: Acting, Singing, and Dancing. I act and sing, so I got a longer audition time. I didn't do the dance audition because that is for true dancers. I'm talking people who've done ballet since birth, and they stand with their feet in either first or fifth position at all times. I was considered "an actor who can move," meaning I can learn and do choreography if it isn't too technical, because I took ballet for a year in elementary school. The dance auditions happen in another ballroom and they are intense as well. Imagine a ballroom full of people with their audition number pinned to their right hip, learning choreography and desperate to make the cut. The whole place looks like a madhouse.

The room that is truly wild is the warm-up room. In every corner of a neighboring ballroom, an actor in job-interview clothes with a number pinned to *their* hip is facing a wall and practicing their monologue or warming up their voice. The truly cocky ones are walking around the room singing and working on their monologues so that every other actor can hear them. The center of the room is filled with dancers warming up and other people just generally stretching their bodies. Picture it: it's Chattanooga 2004, and you walk into a hotel ballroom with two hundred to four hundred people laughing, crying, and fully emoting . . . to no one. To the air! People walking around singing the same song to themselves over and over, or working on their vocal warm-ups. *La, La, La, La, La, La, La* sung at various notes and pitches. Tongue twisters being recited. *She sells seashells by the seashore. . . .*

A dancer leaps past you, followed by another dancer who lifts them up in the air, spins, puts them down, and returns to the line of other dancers. Someone asks if you want to be in the shoulder-massage chain of people sitting on the floor trying to relax and center themselves before their auditions. And then someone with a clipboard pops their head in every few minutes to call out a range of numbers. As those people leave, the next range of numbers files into the room to find their little piece of real estate in this chaos to work on the audition that could change their life. ALSO you are just a nineteen-year-old who is trying to live their dreams and make their family proud. Finally, in all this chaos, I did it. I got one callback from my audition.

It was the morning of the last day, and a lot of the companies were gone. I got a callback from the Main Street Theatre in

Quakertown, Pennsylvania. A callback means the person casting a show wants to see you again because they are interested in hiring you. The callbacks are all in a theater company's hotel room. Not a conference room or a ballroom. A hotel room. You are NEVER alone in the room. There are always other actors who have callbacks, and all the people who work at the theater who are there for the conference. These convention hotels were big, so maybe another system could have been used? One that wasn't so cramped? The callback was in the director's hotel room. Like I said, I wasn't alone. Other employees of the theater and other actors were in a single queen bed hotel room. The director said he called me back because he saw *Ragtime* on my résumé and he was looking to cast the role of "Sarah's friend" and was excited to see I had played it before. I sang a portion of Sarah's friend's solo from the show and he loved it. He said he was out of slots for the season and had to find a way to justify hiring me to the board.

"I have technical theater experience. Does that help?"

"Really!" the director said. "Doing what? Do you have a portfolio?"

"I sure do!" I pulled my portfolio from my self-made Alpha Psi Omega Theatre Honors Society bag. "I have built and painted sets, hung lights, sewn costumes, and I know how to weld."

"You know how to weld?! Wow."

So thanks to my acting AND technical theater training, I got the job!

When it was time to head to Quakertown for the summer, my

mom and brother drove me up to Pennsylvania, and I remember thinking, *Where the hell am I?* There was an Applebee's that had karaoke nights. That's how happening of a town we were in. And you already know about the Walmart. Scandalous! In Georgia, if we were bored, we'd just go walk around in Walmart. In Quakertown, I didn't even have that option.

We worked from sunup past sundown. That season we did four musicals and twelve children's shows. I was in nine of the children's shows, and in five of them I was cast as a bird. One of my most notable roles was the Queen of Hearts in *Alice in Wonderland*, and I *loved* her. Off with their heads, indeed! I was Kanga in *Winnie the Pooh*, and the only problem there was that my friend Micah kept trying to get in my pouch. I played the goose that laid the golden eggs in *Jack and the Beanstalk*. I wore a green hat covered in feathers to let the children know I was a bird, because that was the best prop/costume we could find. The biggest challenge of that role was that I had no lines, so I had to convey all my emotions through squawking. So when Jack came to steal me from the Giant, I had to get the children in the audience to help me wake the Giant up, so I started flapping my arms and yelling *"Kaaaa! Kaaaaa! Kaaaaaaa!"* and motioned to them to join in. Now that I think of it, maybe I should have been honking like a goose, but I was young and had a lot to learn. Little did I know, I would not jump straight from the Quakertown stage into stardom. As you now know, I would hold down (or not) day jobs in used car sales, telemarketing, and stucco before I got my first *real* break.

It was a rigorous schedule. Every morning we had music rehearsal and in the afternoon dance rehearsal for the upcoming show. In the evening we performed the current show. Then after the show we had a children's show rehearsal. Every weekend was a different children's show, but not all of us were cast in those (I was cast the most). Now this was the end of the night for most of the cast. But not for me, since I was an actor-technician.

After all this, I still had to work on lights, wigs, props, and the set. I was being paid a higher rate at $125 because I had two jobs. All the other actors were being paid between seventy-five to a hundred dollars a week. I know the rate seems low, but as summer stock jobs went at the time, it wasn't bad. The theater gave us food and housing. A LOT of other summer stock jobs, even the most prestigious ones, didn't pay and/or didn't give food and housing, which is why you see a lack of diversity in theater. Unless you come from money or your parents are willing to support you for an entire summer, there is no way you can even take on the opportunity you worked so hard for. And it was hard work.

When we opened *Barnum* and performed that show every night, during the day we would rehearse for *How to Succeed in Business Without Really Trying*. And then once *Barnum* was done, we opened *How to Succeed* and then started rehearsing for *Mame*. After *How to Succeed* was done, we opened *Mame* and started rehearsing for *Ragtime*. There was also a weeklong children's theater camp. As the season progressed, the theater was running out of money because the board of trustees had a falling-out and split into two factions. The ones with access to the money no longer wanted to support the theater, so by the end of the season the director was funding the last production with his own savings. None of us got our last paycheck, even though everyone thought *I* did.

I don't know why they thought I got my last check. I never got any special treatment from the director or the board. People just say shit and hope it's true. Did the theater go bankrupt while we were there? Yes. Were our dreams going to be cut short because some rich people changed their mind about funding the arts? Hell no! That is the nature of this industry. Sadly, theaters are always looking for ways to keep their doors open, because they close all the time.

Now, on another note, I know y'all are wondering if *I*, ya girl, hooked up with anyone before the summer was over. And the answer is . . . *drumroll* . . . no. If I did, I would have mentioned it by now! Silly goose. There was no Mechanic, no Dummy, no late-night dates at Applebee's.

So I focused on the work. I played the Bearded Lady in *Barnum*. The director was scared to ask me at first, but I was THRILLED to stick on some facial hair, a colorful dress, and ask audience members to touch my bush. I mean my bushy face! Y'all nasty. My friend Travis played the World's Strongest Man, and I would have to coat him in baby powder before every performance because he sweated so much. His barbells were a pole with two balloons stuck to each side, so I'm not sure why he was so damn sweaty. It's not like he was lifting anything more than twelve ounces. He was one of my best friends that summer, and we still talk to this day. Maybe the baby powder bonded us.

The stage was painted to look like a three-ring circus (actually the stage was so small we had a one-ring circus). If you paint a theater stage where human actors are going to be dancing and leaping, sometimes a Coke wash is used to give the floor some texture so those human actors don't slip and bust their ass. Yes, a Coke wash is a real thing. You pour Coke (the drink) into a bucket and dilute it with water, then you mop it over the paint. That did not happen because the gorgeous paint job wasn't finished until the night before the show opened, and it wasn't dry enough to be coated in a cola solution. Since we couldn't rehearse onstage we had no idea what the conditions would be. When it came time for opening night, well, not even our leather-bottomed Capezio shoes could save us. We asked Chris, the stage manager, why he didn't do the wash. All the dancers in the show asked multiple times and were insisting that it be done.

"It'll be fine," said Chris. Well. It was not fine, Chris.

Not only did we have to walk on this stage—we had to dance the Charleston. Which, if you don't know, is a lot of foot and hand movements. Okay, that is the definition of dancing, but look up a video of the Charleston—it ain't easy. Now remember I'm not a "dancer," I am an actor who can move my body. I can't do full pirouettes and leap across a stage in the splits. We were all wearing floor-length skirts and high-collared shirts, since this was set in the 1800s, and as I danced, I felt myself starting to slip. In fact all of us were slipping and sliding around. Many of my castmates almost fell, but they caught themselves. I, on the other hand, after the fifth successful feat of catching myself, finally lost the battle. I knew I was going to go down, so I spread my arms out at my sides because I needed to fall as gracefully as possible. My left arm tilted toward the floor and my right arm pointed up to the ceiling, so I looked like I was doing a "Ta-da!" move. I knew I was going all the way down, so I folded my legs underneath me. I couldn't just lie there or run offstage and start crying. So I looked up at the boys dancing in the line behind me and mouthed, "Help me up." They nodded and motioned for me to come closer. So I did a barrel roll, laid my arms out flat, and they lifted me. Without missing a beat I popped back up and started doing the Charleston and singing again.

After the song was over and we were backstage changing for the next scene, everyone was making sure that I was okay. One of the girls who was next to me when I fell whispered, "That fall was so graceful."

"Thank you, girl."

"Was that on purpose? Was that new choreography?"

"No, I really fell," I said, laughing. I was embarrassed.

"Well, it looked great!"

The stage manager came to check on me and then said, "All

right, tomorrow before the show we will Coke-wash the stage."

During that summer we lived in the theater. Literally. Some kids stayed in a nearby Red Lion Inn, and a few lodged with members of the theater board, but me and my close friends lived in little dorms in the theater. Compared to the director, who had a gorgeous apartment, we were living in squalor. Okay, squalor is an exaggeration, but it was close. We used to eat what we called orphanage sandwiches, which were lunch meat and cheese on bread. One fine and glorious day I found a stash of butter in the kitchen, and I started cooking up everyone's orphanage sandwiches. What a time to be alive. Hot bologna and cheese. For dinner we usually had undercooked pasta, a meat, and some kind of vegetable. Was it good? Not really. What did I care? I was twenty years old and I was ACTING. Better sandwiches would have been nice, though.

Strange as it seems, I never saw any Quakers in Quakertown. I did see a lot of white Rastas, which was very confusing. During our thirteen weeks there, we did have some drama that was not on the stage. We bonded quickly, since we were all young and stuck together twenty-four hours a day. We would have parties, even though the town had some weird-ass alcohol laws, like you can't walk out of a store carrying more alcohol than you can consume. Made no sense.

One night at a party, this Italian girl with curly black hair who was in the cast came inside crying.

"Girl, what's wrong?" we all asked.

She was shaking and crying. She told us there were three white kids driving around the theater in circles, yelling the N-word and throwing grapes at her. Now, she was Italian, but she was slightly tan with curly hair and it was nighttime, so to some racist Quakertown hooligans she may as well be Black. There were about seven actual Black kids in the program, so all of us ran outside to defend our Italian friend. I remember I had on a tank top that I bedazzled myself. It said *Southern Belle* on the front, and I was wearing a cowboy hat. I was giving full 2004. The car with the grape-throwing racists came around again, yelling and throwing grapes, so I yelled, "I BET you won't stop!" I was tipsy off Smirnoff Ices, so I was ready to GO. I also wanted them to at least slow down so I could get their plate number, which I did. Then we called the cops. This being Quakertown, a cop car showed up real quick. What else did they have to do? Bust up a bad karaoke performance at Applebee's? So the racist car came by and the cop took off after them. He came back about fifteen minutes later, telling us he gave them a ticket for harassment and set a court date.

"It was good they were only throwing grapes," said the cop. "The person in the backseat had a whole fruit basket with apples and bananas."

Oh, well, that was nice of them! People talk about the South being so racist, but of all the times I have been called the N-word, only one time did it happen in the South. It happened multiple times in New York, Los Angeles, Philly, and Colorado. Once in

Georgia a guy with road rage rolled down his window to scream at me, and before he could say anything I yelled, "Wait, are you gonna call me the N-word, you idiot? You think that's gonna bother me?!" I started laughing, which *really* pissed him off. I'm glad he didn't try to kill me. So maybe if he'd had his way, that would have been the second time in the South I was called the N-word. I'll never know.

That night gave us a little real-life drama, courtesy of some Yankee racists whose weapon of choice was a fruit basket. I did have a dramatic moment on the stage when I was in the musical *How to Succeed in Business Without Really Trying*. There's a song in the show called "Paris Original" about a fancy dress from Paris. All twelve girls in the scene are supposed to have on the same dress, but there was not a matching dress in my size.

Instead of having me sit the scene out, the director looked at me and said, "Honey, you are the only one who will have a Paris original."

Okay, bitch. I was all in.

So I had a gold-and-pink brocade dress and a red beehive wig. I came out at the end of the number and gave a haughty, "Humph!" I slid my gloves on and strutted off that stage in a way that said, "Yeah, bitches. Y'all shop at Old Navy and I have BROCADE." It was a center stage moment and it heightened the scene with a little humor. When I thanked the director, he just said, "Honey, I have vision." And yes, he did.

Now, I got plenty of drama on the stage, but since everybody but me was flirting and fucking all summer long, I needed more. Thanks to Peter, Mark, and Greg, I got my fill.

So Peter had a huge crush on Mark, who was cute as hell. Everyone loved Mark. But Mark was not giving Peter the time of day. So Peter started dating Greg because Greg really liked him. Basically Greg liked Peter as much as Peter liked Mark, and Peter was happy to have the attention, since Mark was giving him none!

One night, me and my friends Kelli and Leo (who I still gossip with) were sitting on the stage at one in the morning chitchatting, and all of a sudden we heard yelling coming from the bathroom. We got quiet, ducked down, and shared various excited glances and clutching-of-pearl moments. Is this? Yes. It might be . . . DRAMA! Thank you, Jesus!

We sneaked into the bathroom to find out what the hell was going on, and we heard Peter and Greg arguing. And when I say sneaked, I mean military-style crawled across the floor and into the dressing room to get a better look and be able to hear, until realizing that we were too close and would be found out. At one point Peter looked over to the dressing room like he heard something, and we realized we had to move because at any minute one of them could come storming out the single bathroom they were openly arguing in. After that, me, Leo, and Kelli went into the nearby ladies' room and stood on toilets in neighboring stalls to listen in. Got all that?

Well, it turns out that Peter had kissed someone else. Greg

kept asking who it was, and finally Peter blurted it out.

"Mark! I kissed Mark."

"What? What do you mean?!?"

"I KISSED Mark, OKAY?!"

Oh shit! We tried not to squeal or breathe. Except for Leo, who let out the shortest yelp of "Whaaaa . . ." in human history until he slapped his own hand over his mouth. We were getting ALL THE TEA! This was high tea served boiling hot. It was a Southern day in Texas!

"I only dated you because I felt bad for you," said Peter to Greg.

The nerve. The audacity. The unmitigated gall. Greg was a cute boy and very nice and didn't need Peter's pity. Greg replied, "Really? If it wasn't for me you would have spent the summer alone and sad hoping for Mark to finally pay attention to you!"

"Well, he did, and we are gonna start dating."

"It's the end of the summer."

"So?"

"Why did he wait until the end of the summer? He doesn't really like you. I do!"

"Well, he is who I wanted all along."

Now we were all mad at Peter and felt very bad for Greg because Peter was being a piece of shit to him. This was better than Walmart! After Greg stormed out and Peter stomped away, me, Leo, and Kelli scurried back to the stage, our hearts pumping with the adrenaline that comes from some GOOD-ASS TEA.

We went back into the theater and lay out on the stage.

"Girl!"

"Girl!"

"Giiiiiirl!!!"

This was too fucking good. It was the biggest scandal we got all summer. And we spilled all the way to the end of summer. Good tea requires visual aids, lots of hand motions, a few props, and an audience that is hungry for drama.

That summer, I was performing for every audience back in Quakertown. Adults. Children. Castmates. I am always ready to perform. I am still that woman who barrel-rolls herself across a stage and is lifted back up to dance the Charleston instead of crawling off the stage, defeated. Most of all, friends, I am *always* here to spill (and share) the tea—onstage and in real life. It's my destiny.

ACKNOWLEDGMENTS

First, thank you to the Father, the Son, and Holy Ghost for continuing to bless me and my family. My mother, Mary Ann Hill, for all her love and support, and always making sure I stayed focused on what I wanted in life. My brother, Lawrence Sloan, for all his love and support. My papa, Michael Dowe, for always taking care of me. Sometimes you gotta go people-watch at a Pappadeaux on Valentine's Day.

My family in Atlanta: Antonio Darden and his family, the Bahena family, the Ramirez family, and the Alvarado family. Thank you for blessing me to be your Hija, Hermana, Prima, Tia, and Sobrina. Special thanks to my niece Citllali for being the best assistant and niece I could ever have.

Thank you to the teachers that saw me as a person and helped to nurture me.

To Big Kenney Johnson for seeing me as a comic and teaching me how to write a joke and to be myself onstage. To Gabi Gavrilla for letting me take thirteen days off work to do comedy festivals and NACAs to become a full-time comic. To the Atlanta acting and stand-up comedy community for supporting me. To the LA and NYC stand-up communities for embracing me. Thank you especially to David Perdue, Lace Larrabee, Shalewa Sharpe, Madison Shepard, Danielle Perez, Ben Bergman, Joe Kelley, Tone Bell, Baron Vaughn, Sarah Tiana, Roy Wood Jr., Josh Johnson, Tiffany Haddish, and Trevor Noah.

A huge thanks to Michelle Buteau, who encouraged me and told me that I do have the ability and life experience to write this book.

Thank you to my manager, Reg, for changing my life, pushing me when I wanted to say no, supporting me when I said yes, and being a friend. You got me out of the stucco factory, lol.

Thank you to Tigerman Management, Levity Entertainment, APA, UTA, Kirkland Productions, Reign Agency, TruTV, Comedy Central, Brenau University, Aurora Theatre, *The Great North*, and *The Daily Show.*

Thank you to Judi-Brown Marmel, J. P. Buck, Conan O'Brien, Amy Poehler, Eva Longoria, Dina Gachman, Maureen Taran, Charlene Conley, Enid Seymore, Kat Eves, Tara Copeland, Erin Tonge, Wendy Molyneux, Lizzie Molyneux, Karen Horne, Ann-Carol Pence, Anthony Rodriguez, and Al Stilo.

And from the Andscape family, thank you so much to: Tonya Agurto, Jennifer Levesque, Amy King, Steph Sumulong, Alex Serrano, Ann Day, Daneen Goodwin, Guy Cunningham, Meredith Jones, Aliya King Neil, and Olivia Zavitson.

© Bronson Farr

DULCÉ SLOAN is one of the sharpest, fastest-rising voices in comedy. *Bust* magazine calls her "comedy gold," while *IndieWire* describes her as "a fresh and unique voice in the world of stand-up comedy." She was included in *Variety*'s prestigious Top Ten Comedians to Watch list, and *Slink* magazine just crowned her "The New Queen of Comedy." *Rolling Stone* recently hailed her as one of the Ten Comedians You Need to Know. As a correspondent on Comedy Central's *The Daily Show with Trevor Noah* since 2017, her segments have garnered millions of views. Dulcé stars as one of the voices on the animated FOX series *The Great North*, joining an ensemble of comedy heavyweights, including Will Forte, Jenny Slate, Nick Offerman, and Megan Mullally. When Dulcé's Comedy Central Presents stand-up special premiered on Comedy Central, the *New York Times* included the half hour in their Best Comedy of 2019 roundup.